GW00597349

TWO YORKSHIRE SOLDIERS

Family Heroes 1914-18

Andy Volans

This edition published in Great Britain in 2014 by
Farthings Publishing
8 Christine House
1 Avenue Victoria
SCARBOROUGH
YO11 2QB
UK

http://www.Farthings-Publishing.com
E-mail: queries@farthings.org.uk

ISBN 978-1-291- 87125 - 8

June 2014 (e)

DEDICATION

This book is dedicated to all those ordinary men and women who performed extraordinary feats of courage during the First World War, and to their families who keep their memory alive.

ACKNOWLEDGEMENTS

To Jane Rowntree, Herbert's Niece; and Kath Sedman, Charles' daughter, who are the guardians for their mementoes, and to the Imperial War museum for the pictures where indicated.

The front cover depicts poppies growing
in a field at Ypres.

CONTENTS

INTRODUCTION

These stories come from two small collections kept within our families to remember our relatives who served in the First World War.

The first one I saw when I was first introduced to my wife's mother, Jane. On the table was a Princess Mary Christmas box, one of which was sent to all troops in service in December 1914. These were filled with either chocolate or cigarettes. This tin contained the attestation papers and letters along with photographs of Herbert, her great uncle who had fought in the Great War as a Grenadier Guard.

Herbert's Tin

The second box belonged to my Great Uncle. It contains his medals, his NCO whistle, the bullet that brought him home and several letters and newspaper cuttings.
There were a few family tales that went with these items and I wondered how much I could find to flesh out the stories and see how real they were likely to be.
From these starting points, via the regimental histories, it was possible to identify where and when these two ordinary men performed the extraordinary feats of bravery that still live on in our folk memory.

Charles' Tin

These are their stories...

***

CHAPTER 1

1918

On the morning of the 11th of November, 1918, two Yorkshire soldiers realised that they had survived, they had a future they could plan for.
In Fulford Barracks, York, Company Sergeant Major, Charles Volans 36, of the 3/5th West Yorkshire Battalion, currently serving with the Army Service Corps, heard the church bells peal, announcing the end of hostilities.

The Guards at the Porte de France, Maubeuge

In Maubeuge, in Northern France, Private Herbert Pollington MM, age 22, of 3 Company, 3 Battalion Grenadier Guards, sat on the wall outside the Porte de France. He and his mates were resting at the southern gate of Maubeuge doing what soldiers always do when left to themselves; sitting, smoking, drinking tea, and chatting with the Padre, Capt. Phillimore, who was circulating amongst the troops as he had done for 4 years, this time, organizing the church parade that was scheduled for later that day.

As 11 o-clock approached, to the north near Mons, the firing intensity increased, almost as if the artillery wanted to use up all their spare ammunition. If the Armistice failed, some poor lads from the infantry were going to suffer some very heavy fatigues carrying up the shells for the re-supply.

With military precision quiet spread along the battle line at 11am, leaving an unnatural peace, not heard for 4 years. As the roar of gunfire settled, the ordinary sounds appeared, the talk of the town's folk as they came out of their cellars into the street and the clatter of horses coming up the pave road from Longueville bringing the Field artillery forward to support the line whilst the Germans withdrew across the French border into Germany.

This was their war...

***

CHAPTER 2

THE WORLD THE WAR CHANGED

Above: The Volans Family at Duncombe Place, York

Charles was born on 30th May 1883 in the parish of Bootham, York. He was the penultimate child of 11 of William George Bell Volans and his wife Ann Arnold of 4/5 Duncombe Place. The last baby born was Frederick Alfred Ernest (Grandfather to the current Volans clan).
William George Bell was a successful businessman, given the size of their house at Duncombe place, very successful, within the printing industry.

Herbert was born in 1896 in Northallerton, North Yorkshire, the son of William (a boot maker) and Mary (a baker) Pollington. By the time of the 1911 census, the family had moved to Melbourne Place, Sowerby, Thirsk, where William was a boot repairer, and were living in Victoria Avenue. By this time the family consisted of his parents, Herbert, his brother Alfred Baden, sister Jessie and baby brother Harry.

Above: Mary and Herbert Pollington

This was the world of Empire. Queen Victoria had ruled from 1837 and in 1900 was still on the throne. Great Britain had not been involved in a European war for almost 100 years, since the defeat of Napoleon at Waterloo in 1815.

As a result of the French losing at Waterloo, the British had taken control of the many French military bases and colonies around the world, and had used them to develop the Empire that coloured the school atlas red.

There had been wars but these had been far away such as in the Crimea 60 years ago or in the colonies, and they had mostly fallen the British way, or at least they had, according to the newspapers, the most recent being the two Boer wars,1880 to 1881 and 1890 to 1892. During the second Boer war, there had been the famous siege of Mafeking in 1890, when Baden Powell's cunning and tricks had protected the town against overwhelming Boer forces for 217 days until British reinforcements relieved them and defeated the Boer forces.

The tales of these exploits were embellished and spread around the Empire by writers such as Rudyard Kipling, and the papers raised Robert Baden Powell to almost Heroic status back at home.

There was limited democracy. Men could vote if they were over 30 and owned their homes. Women had little independence, had difficulty in owning their own houses and of course could not vote.

Liberal views were growing in the prosperous middle classes within the UK. People like the Rowntrees of Scarborough were bringing Boer politicians to Britain and trying to show the other sides of the Colonial wars, but in general, being born English was to be born part of the naturally ruling race.

In 1900, at the age of 17, Charles started working as a clerk and to give himself some excitement he joined the Yorkshire Volunteers (1st Volunteer Battalion), a part time force that had been founded in 1859 as an auxiliary force expected to protect the country from invasion. The troops met at local barracks, in this case at Fulford in York, and trained in the traditional military skills of square bashing, marching, rifle drill and shooting at the firing range.

Every year, they got to spend two weeks in camp on exercise.

The force was locally recruited, supervised and funded. Politically, the force was poorly supported by the War Ministry and Parliament in general. Often the troops could not get time off work and also would not get their expenses paid to get to training or to camp but despite this, they were considered to be sufficiently expert that three Battalions from the Volunteers, in particular, the Halifax Rifle Brigade, had been out to serve in South Africa in 1900. It is likely that this chance for travel and excitement was part of the reason that Charles had joined in March 1900.

In 1901 Victoria died, passing the crown to her son, Edward VII until his death in 1910 when George V took the throne.

In 1905 it was being discussed whether a volunteer force would be able to supply the troops needed in an emergency or whether it would be better to go straight to compulsory enlistment of civilians, something that was not considered “how the English did things”.

By 1907, the War Ministry was seeing signs of impending war in Europe and felt that the Volunteer Force should be modernised and reorganised resulting in the 1907 Haldane Act, forming the Territorial Forces, based on County Towns and supported by National funds. The West Riding Association was set up in 1908 with a target of 18,300 troops of all ranks. At this time there were 414 officers and 9683 other ranks, just over half the requirement.

On the 9th May 1908, Charles was transferred into the new force as a Sergeant 322, of the 1st (Territorial) Battalion of the 5th West Yorkshire Regiment.

5th W. Yorks on parade 1911 outside Duncombe Place, York

In July 1908 they performed their first parade where the records reported that their equipment was obsolete and completely unsuited to modern service. Their first Divisional camp was held that summer in Redcar.

Over the next few years there was a steady battle between the Association and the War Office to obtain funding, modern equipment and uniforms. There were regular mobilisation exercises that showed the gap between the need and supply of weapons, artillery, uniforms, boots, horses, wagons and tack.

In 1911 there was a scare at national level when the German gun boat, Panther, sailed into Agadir threatening the French forces there and making it possible that Britain would have to join France in a war against Germany. After this, supplies and finance started to be made available to the Associations to allow the troops to attend training since a trial mobilisation had again failed to supply sufficient troops or equipment.

In 1911 Charles paraded past the family home in York (previous page) as part of the Sunday Parade in tribute to General Gordon of Khartoum.

***

CHAPTER 3

THE START OF THE WAR

Germany, or rather the Kaiser, his generals and courtiers, wanted to expand German influence. They wanted colonies like the British and French and they wanted more of the disputed Alsace region, near Switzerland that was currently shared with France.

Kaiser Wilhelm II was a nephew of Queen Victoria. He had replaced his pro-British father who had died after only 3 months on the throne in 1881.

Otto von Bismark, the leading German statesman for many years, had created "Greater Germany" in 1871, and by 1879 had arranged the alignment of Austria – Hungary, previously bitter enemies of Germany / Prussia, with the German Kaiser.

Arch Duke Ferdinand the head of the Austrian state was the apparent heir to the Kaiser's throne over the Germanic states.

By 1890 the Kaiser had retired Bismark and unrestrained, the Kaiser had almost absolute power.

In December 1897, Bismarck warned the Kaiser about the dangers of government policy based on the intrigues of courtiers and militarists. Bismarck's last warning was:

"The crash will come twenty years after my departure if things go on like this. One day the great European War will come out of some damned foolish thing in the Balkans".

Known within the European royal family, (and the UK press) as Little Willie, the Kaiser had suffered trauma at birth leaving him with a withered left arm and according to diplomatic sources, some concerns about his sanity.

He behaved erratically, was immature, and had an unpleasant sense of humour that centred on painful and humiliating practical jokes. He loved weapons and military pomp and would dress in flamboyant military uniforms of his own designs and, it was whispered, was possibly a homosexual.

Like the UK, there was a civilian arm of the Army in Germany, but unlike England, the German Military machine reached deep into the public heart.

The different regions of Greater Germany, such as Saxony, Bavaria, Hanover and Prussia, supported armies and in every region the role of a soldier was considered an honourable duty.

One could first wear a uniform at 17 and you were not free of service until you were 45. However, unlike in England, where your Army service was seen as slightly odd, one gained standing and political and social advantage within Germany by serving in either the regular or the reserve army.

The assassination of Archduke Ferdinand and his wife, in Sarjevo in 1914 by Gavrilo Princip a Serbian freedom activist, turned out to be the event predicted by Bismark. It was seen as a challenge to the Austro-Hungarian Empire and with German connivance a declaration of war was made on Serbia, hoping to split the long standing Entente between France, Russia and England since it was assumed that the Russians would support Serbia, but France and Britain would not.

Such a plan to break up the Entente had been around since a military conference in1912.

The Russians responded as expected giving Germany the excuse to support Austria-Hungary and mobilise themselves.

Since the initial Russian moves had not stopped Austria-Hungary's threat to Serbia, the Czar ordered a full Army mobilisation.

The French were understandably concerned about the German mobilisation against Russia, and expected them to use this mobilization as an excuse for further activity in the Alsace region where France and Germany had suffered generations of border disputes and consequently they felt that they were compelled to mobilise in order to support Russia under their Entente of understanding.

The Germans did not want to fight a war on two fronts and so needed to neutralise France quickly so that they could concentrate on defeating the vast if disorganised Russian armies in the East. Also they wanted ports on the Atlantic Coast to free their battleship squadrons from the limits imposed by the Baltic Sea on their main deep-water port near Hamburg.

The French had fortified the borders between themselves and Germany so the German strategy, the Schlieffen plan, was to pass around these, through the eastern region of Belgium and so sweep down onto Paris and to knock France out of the war.

The English had treaties with France and Russia declaring mutual aid in the event of a third party attacking them. In addition, Britain had a separate treaty with Belgium supporting its independence.

In the past, the English had supported from afar using the Navy, and planned on only entering any actual land fighting when the European armies had tired each other out.

However, in this modern era, the presence of a powerful German fleet on the channel coast would allow easy access for German Dreadnoughts to the trade lines that supported the British Empire. With the Germans restricted to their Baltic homeland ports, the British Navy was able to bottle them up by controlling the North Sea, so it would not be in the British interests to let France or Belgium fall into German hands.

Once Germany invaded Belgium, the British Government would have the need and the excuse to respond.

As the risk of war became more likely in 1914, the British Government needed a soldier capable of the massive task of organising for a European war.

Field Marshal Lord Kitchener had spent his professional career fighting imperial wars for England. He was persuaded to come out of retirement by Prime Minister Asquith.

Kitchener recognised that the mass armies and modern technology available to France and Germany were likely to mean an extended war of attrition and so England needed to mobilise the resources of the whole Empire to tilt the balance in favour of the allies.

On 1st August 1914, the Germans declared war on France, their idea being, to take Paris quickly, removing France as threat to them in the West, and so allow them to concentrate on Russia. On the same day, the German Government demanded passage through Belgium to allow them to sweep around the French border fortifications onto Paris from the north. Albert I, the King of Belgium responded by asking England to honour their Treaty to support Belgium in the event of invasion.

At this time, Charles was in Scarborough at the annual camp at the Barracks above North Bay, with the 5th Battalion West Yorkshire (York) Territorial Battalion under Lt. Col. C.E. Wood. Also at the camp were the 6th West Yorks. (Bradford), the 7th and 8th Leeds Rifles and the West Yorks. Rifles (Leeds) along with 1/1st West Riding Casualty Clearing station. On August Bank Holiday Saturday (1st), in the afternoon, a motorcycle dispatch rider arrived at the barracks with sealed orders calling on all the Battalions to mobilise immediately and return to their Headquarters. Consequently the Troops packed immediately and late at night marched through Scarborough to the station, cheered on by the town's folk coming out on the streets in their nightclothes.

On the 2nd, Germany invaded Luxembourg and then crossed the Belgian border on the 3rd of August. On the 4th Britain honoured its agreements and formally declared war on Germany in support of 'plucky little Belgium' as the newspapers screamed in banner headlines.

On the 7th the French attacked towards Mulhouse, near Switzerland, in the disputed and currently German held part of the Alsace region, precisely as the German plans had predicted.

Between the 12th and 18th of August, the British Expeditionary Force successfully crossed the channel, mostly during the night to avoid the German submarines that were presumed to be active in the channel.

The force consisted of 48 Battalions, each of about 1000 men.

This constituted the majority of the Regular troops available in the UK at that time.

The British Expeditionary Force was transported by train to Maubeuge from where they marched north to meet the German Advance at Mons in Belgium. Here the small "Contemptible Army", in the Kaiser's words, was driven into a fighting retreat.

This was a traditional set of open battles, little different in style and tactics from those fought against Napoleon 100 years before, but on a larger scale with 7 German Armies pushing against 6 French Armies and the British Force.

In September, the allied armies held the German advance on the River Marne and then pushed them back north, trying to get around the Western flank of the German forces in what became a race to the sea near Nieuport in Belgium that only stopped when the Belgians opened the sea sluices and released the waters into the low lying polder land there, flooding it and making an impenetrable flank defence for both sides.

Once this drive stopped, the troops on both sides started to dig in, creating trenches, initially just traditional, military, shallow protective ditches; but later developing into the complexes for which the War is remembered.

The Western Front

By Christmas 1914 the trench line had stabilised and was developing in complexity from the coast to the Swiss border in the Alsace.

The British Expeditionary force was centred along a line from around Ypres in southern Belgium to Argentieres in Northern France, with the Belgian Army on the far left near the sea, and a French Army on the left and right British flanks.

***

CHAPTER 4

MOBILISATION OF THE TROOPS

When Charles and his Battalion arrived at their Fulford barracks they were renamed 1/5th West Yorkshire Battalion, being the First Line Battalion of the 5th Regiment, since they were most trained and best armed.

Their task now, was to bring the Battalion onto a war footing, doubling the troop numbers up to full strength (1007 Officers and men, divided into an HQ Company of 66 led by Lt. Col. Wood supported by a Major, and 4 fighting Companies commanded by a Major or Captain, A to D, each made up of 4 platoons under a Lieutenant, each of which was further divided into 4 sections of 12 men under the control of an Non-Commissioned Officer (of which Charles was one).

A Co

ROLL OF No 2 Section

Regtl. No.	RANK AND NAME.	Remarks
	No 2 Platoon	
	No 8 Section	
Sgt	C. Volans	
Lce Cpl	Moore	
"	Appleton	Signaller
Pte	Dinsdale	
"	Dungate	
"	Deans	
"	Harrison J.R.	O.S.
"	Stubbs W.H.	
"	Sturdy F.	Cook
"	Liffitt	
"	Fairbairn	
"	Watson	
"	Fose	
"	Dyson	M.G.
"	Goodwin	Transport
"	Smith W.E.	Cook

Section book, August 1914

They also had to acquire enough weapons, boots, uniforms, tents and equipment including vehicles, wagons, field kitchens, stores and 60 horses to allow them to operate in the field, initially for defensive roles in England, but rapidly, it became apparent that the British Expeditionary Force in France was going to need reinforcements if the German assault was to be held.

To assist, on the 7th of August, Kitchener issued an appeal for 100,000 volunteers for the Army. Within 5 months 1.2 million men had volunteered. They wanted to be in the adventure, and thought that the war would be over within a year, (Kitchener had always planned for a three year war).

Because the army had not expected such a massive response, they were not ready to place all these men and many were billeted in private homes or makeshift camps whilst waiting for uniforms and formal training.

In the early days of August, the Territorial Commanders were asked for volunteers to serve abroad and within weeks over 90% had signed up for overseas duties.

Recruitment was started by the Territorial Association and within a month the Yorkshire Association had sufficient recruits to form 2 further training lines of Battalions for the Regiment.

In the first weeks, the 1/1st West Riding Casualty Clearing Station (CCS) was mobilised to full strength and was deployed by the end of October, arriving in the support town of Poperinghe in time to treat the wounded from the First Battle of Ypres as the 7th CCS. At the end of November it moved to Merville, setting up in the Monastery of St. Joseph where it served the battlefields of Neuve Chapelle, Aubers and Festubert.

Over the next few months, the Territorial Battalions underwent intensive training in fighting and manoeuvres and then, as the pattern of the war changed, they practiced trench construction and wiring.

Meanwhile, Herbert had become 18 in October 1914. He was a farm labourer. His world was heavy manual labour with the hope of the odd pint when he could afford it.

Mind you that pint was risky. His father was a strict Methodist, and had once thrown a metal boot last at him and his brother Alfred when they came in smelling of beer. The heavy last had flown through the window into the street narrowly missing passers-by.

For an 18 year old in this world, he could stay working the fields or he could join the big adventure offered by Kitchener's poster. He could fight for his country.

On 14th November 1914, Three months after the call to arms, Herbert went in to Thirsk and enlisted, specifying service with the Grenadier Guards, the foremost Infantry Regiment of the Regular Army.

There is a family story that Herbert joined up to get away from his father, who was said to be a bully and tried to impose his teetotal views on his boys.

If Herbert had joined up to avoid his father it is unlikely that he would have waited to join the Regular Army, and the most prestigious regiment in it.

He could have joined his mates in the local Battalion of the West Yorkshire regiment, the Alexandra, Princess of Wales Own Yorkshire Regiment, but Herbert had ambition and wanted 'to do his bit' and he chose a regiment most likely to be in the midst of it.

His enlistment medical shows why he was acceptable to the Guards:

'He is tall, at 5 foot 10 inches, and therefore suitable to be a Royal Guard. However, despite his height, he only weighs 145 lbs (10 stone 5 lb, 65Kg) and has a 34 inch chest (that he can push up to 36 inches by a deep breath in).'

This was not unusual for the era. Most young men at that time were very slight, indeed many were rejected in the early years of the war because they were so small and considered unfit for military service. It was only later in the war that many previously rejected men were taken in to replace the fallen.

'He has brown eyes, brown hair and fresh complexion and described his civilian job as a farm labourer.

He also claims to be a Wesleyan, a branch of the Methodists very popular amongst the working class and also theoretically, teetotal.'

Following enlistment he went down to London for training at Wellington Barracks, with the 3rd Battalion of the Grenadier Guards, rather than joining the Reserve Battalion for training, as became the practice later in the war.

For 9 months, the Third Battalion of was retained in London to act as Guard for the King at Buckingham Palace. The Official Regimental record suggests that there were political reasons why an elite Battalion was retained in London when all the rest of the Regular Army was in France. It was said that the constitution required two regular Battalions to be in England, one to guard the King and one for Parliament.

The King declined to keep his Battalion and that left the Third Battalion Grenadier Guards as the sole regular army presence in the UK. There was, of course, the fact that with the bulk of the army engaged in France, there was the need to have a regular army presence to defend England if the Germans should try to invade.

Consequently they were expected to be ceremonial but due to the war were allowed to parade in field Khaki rather than the traditional red uniforms with Bearskins.

Their uniforms were of course of better quality and better fitted than the standard issue.

During this time, the Officers and NCO's were rotated through units in the Front line in France to gain experience in preparation for deployment.

***

CHAPTER 5

THE ARMY of 1914 to 1918

The British forces in France were divided into a number of Armies.

Each Army was administered by two Army Corps which were based on a region of the trenches and controlled all the military activities in that area.

Each Corps had Brigades of Artillery made up of Heavy, Light and Field guns and a Machine Gun Brigade. These were of varying sizes depending on the current activity in that region.

There was a supporting network of Medical, Dental and Veterinary hospitals, Veterinary Corps and Engineering units along with the supply service, the Army Service Corps. This was all supported by a number of Labour Units (often Chinese) and Military Police and guards who controlled the rear areas.

Each Corps contained two Divisions, that were originally planned to stay within their Corps but as the war progressed the Divisions were moved between Corps areas for rest or to perform specific tasks.

By January 1915, the Territorial Force had been organised into a Division, ready to replace the duties of the Imperial Service Division as it left Britain to support the troops in France.

The 49th Territorial Division, fielding 12 Infantry Battalions, each of about 1000 men was divided into two infantry Brigades. It also contained 4 Brigades of Royal Field Artillery, a Trench Mortar Brigade, the Ammunition Train to support them, a brigade of Royal Engineers, a Battalion of Pioneers, the 19th Lancashire Fusiliers, who's role was supplying building skills to support the Divisional area, The Medical Team with 2 Field

Ambulances. Supporting the logistics of all these troops was the Divisional Royal Army Service Corps with about 500 men, along with Military Police, Veterinary Services and a number of smaller specialised services. In all about 20,000 men would make up the Division if the units were up to strength. Consequently a Corps would be about 40,000 men and an army about 80,000 fighting men plus supporting services.

No. 2 Section

Regtl. No.	RANK AND NAME	Married or Single	Date of Enlistment or recommencement of Service	Age on Enlistment	Term of Service	Religion	G. C. Badges	Class Service or Proficiency Pay	Musketry Classification	No. of Rifle	No. of Rifle Bolt	No. of Equipment	In Possession Perm. Pass
1414	~~Sgt. Pawl E.~~	M	Apr/[illegible]	23	4	C.E.				233	157	264	
[illegible]	Cpl. Hood	M	Feb/09	28	4	W.				424	27792	514	
1287	Pte. Bradley W. S.	S	Aug/12	17	4	W.				8191	[illegible]	10	
[illegible]	L/Cpl. Appleton	S	Jan/10	17	4	C.E.				6940	9377	304	
[illegible]	Pte. Dinsdale C.	S	Aug/14	23	4	C.E.				095	40846	302	
1553	[illegible]	S	Jan/14	18	4	C.E.				171	[illegible]	371	

Section book –April 1915

In the Section Book, carried by Charles during his time with the division, the earliest date identifiable is 27th February 1915. During this time the note book records 1414 Sgt. Pawl, checking the readiness of 2 Platoon, B Company which originally has 65 men in it. It originally has 4 sections, 5-8, with 322 Sgt C. Volans in charge of 8 section.

At some stage before deployment, the Company becomes A Company and Charles becomes section leader of 2 Section, replacing Sgt. Pawl.

The section book contains records of checking; boots, rifles, (Charles' rifle is number 75854) and ammunition shortages. There is also a record of him being short of a blanket at one time. We can also see which of the troops are retained in York to support the training Battalion (2/5th West Yorks).

The Terriers go to war

Between 12th and 16th of April, the Territorial Division started towards France.

We know that Charles was still in England on the 14th because he receives 'good luck' telegrams from family members on that day addressed to him in A Company and giving an address on 173 Ropery Walk, (now Ropery Road) Gainsborough, Lincolnshire. Presumably the Battalion embarked from Folkstone, the Division embarking from there as well as Avonmouth and Southampton, to reduce the chances of submarines destroying a whole Division.

Charles, with the 1/5th arrived in Boulogne and was then transported to Mervilles (where the Divisional Casualty Clearing Station is already in place) north of Lens, and west of Armentieres. Here they joined 4th Corps, of 1st Army under Lt. General Sir Henry Rawlinson. The 49th Division sets up its HQ in the town and on the 18th and 19th April, officers and senior NCO's, presumably including Charles, were taken up to the line facing the Aubers Ridge, in the Neuve Chappelle area, for instruction on trench life under the care of the 23rd and 25th Brigade of the 8th Division.

The 49th Division was expected to take control of the Front line between Le Bridoux and Cordonnerie Farm so as to allow the 7th and 8th Divisions to lead the assault. Once the German Line had been taken, the 49th Division was to advance and hold the new Allied front line.

The Army that the division was joining had been severely pressed by the First Battle of Ypres in November 1914, where every reserve of the professional Army had been used and destroyed in holding the German assault on the City when the Germans had hoped to split the English forces from the French and thereby gain access to the rail links behind, allowing them to gain the coast behind the English denying them access to the supply ports as well as driving down onto Paris from the North.

Aubers Ridge

The success of the Allies in preventing the breakthrough had been at massive cost and consequently the Armies facing the Germans for the new spring offensives were made up of the Territorials' and the first of the Battalions from Kitchener's New Volunteer Army.

This First major assault of 1915, described as the Battles of Neuve Chappelle (the largest village in the line) was against the German held Aubers ridge lying to the north of Neuve Chappelle, and started on Sunday May 9th.

The guns that the 49th Division had brought with them, were all ex-Boer War weapons, but were welcomed anyway, due to the sad lack of artillery for the assault. Another problem was the shortage in numbers and poor quality of the shells that could be issued. The re-supply of ammunition from England had not yet moved up to full speed as it did under Lloyd George later in 1915, in time for the Somme offensive of 1916. Consequently when the 8th Division came out of their trenches they found the wire in No-man's land uncut and they could not get through to the German lines.

The view of this battle by the enthusiastic Territorial Force was printed in the Weekly Supplement to the Yorkshire Herald on 14th May 1915 (next page) when a letter from Charles to his parents was used in a stirring piece, obviously designed to bring in volunteers to the Territorials and New Army that was recruiting vigorously at the time. The letter to his father William (WGB) who was a printer by trade, had been passed on to the editor of the paper.

'Away from the trenches in Northern France comes a message today from York lads to York lads, a message written under a baptism of fire, one that tells not of causes of war, but of crowded hours of glorious life. *'You could almost imagine'* says the writer, *'that you were at the Gala on a night, what with the whistling of the bullets and the illumination of their star shells, which they throw up to see if they can sight some of our close cropped 'nappers' peeping over the parapet of the trenches, instead of which they get a volley which must make them think they are better below.'*

The Yorkshire Spirit

The story from which the extract is taken tells of the life of York Territorials across the channel during the past three weeks and is recounted by Sergeant Volans, of A Company 1/5th West Yorkshire Regiment, in letters to his parents Mr. and Mrs Volans of 4 and 5 Duncombe place, and to his sister. In them he seems to have no thought of self, and one cannot fail to admire the human bulldog British note underlying the terse paragraph in one of the letters to his father, *'I am glad to hear you are bearing up bravely during my absence and can quite understand you having rather anxious moments at times, but all I can stay is stick it'.*

The lengthy article goes on to describe life in the rear trenches with airships floating about and guns heard quite distinctly *'which break the monotony.'*

It describes how on the night of the 4th of May the Battalion set off from its billets to march 10 miles in pouring rain. Everyone was drenched and slept fully clothed (and wet) in dugouts on arrival in the trenches awaiting surprise attack. As they approached the trenches they were met with a hail of bullets but no one was hit although they had to walk bent double to avoid injury.

By Friday they had only suffered a few causalities, one severe, from a sniper bullet to the chest. On Friday night there are few shells that do little harm landing in unoccupied trenches.

'The spirit in which the 'Terriers' opposed the enemy is revealed in an excerpt from Sargt. Volans' letter *'we all turn out and open fire on the Germans at 2.30 every morning, as this is the time that they might try and break through our lines, as they are only 500 yards from us, but they'll get their jackets warmed if they start doing the dirt on the 5th.'*

MAY 14. 1915.

YORK TERRITORIALS.

FIRST NEWS FROM FIRING LINE.

HEROIC CONDUCT OF THE 5th WEST YORKS.

STIRRING STORY OF SHOT AND SHELL.

Away from the trenches in Northern France comes a message to-day from York lads to York lads, a message written under a baptism of fire, one that tells not of causes of war, but of crowded hours of glorious life. "You could almost imagine," says the writer, "that you were at the Gala on a night, what with the whistling of the bullets, and the illumination of their star shells, which they throw up to see if they can sight some of our close cropped 'nappers' peeping over the parapets of the trenches, instead of which they get a volley which must make them think they are better below." Inspiring words written on the top of a mess tin, in a little dug-out where you can hear the crack of the sniper's rifle and the whistle of the bullet overhead, and the stern reply of the artillery giving the enemy a surprise packet in the way of a shell, just to let them know that the 5th West Yorkshires never sleep. Aye, words that have all the elements of the true recruiter, sentences that will burn into the minds of many a young fellow before the day is out, and lead him to embody in action the noble phrase—"'Tis a far far better thing I go to do than I have ever done before."

THE YORKSHIRE SPIRIT

The story from which the extract is taken, tells of the life of York Territorials across the Channel during the past three weeks, and is recounted by Sergeant Vollans, of "A" Company 1st 5th West Yorkshire Regiment, in letters to his parents, Mr. and Mrs. Vollans, of 4 and 5, Duncombe-place, and to his sister. In these he seems to have no thought of self, and one cannot fail to admire the human bull-dog British note underlying a terse paragraph in one of the letters to his father, "I am glad to hear you are bearing up bravely during my absence, and can quite understand you having rather anxious moments at times, but all I can say is stick it." "Stick it" is the dominant note not only of the individual, but of the regiment, and many should be the recruits who will decide to help them to "stick it" by responding to the clarion call, not only of King and country, but of kith and kin and friend and of the adventurous life.

FIERCE FIGHTING.

Which of them can but be stirred by the word picture, depicting first the incidents of life in the rear trenches, of airships floating about and guns heard quite distinctly "which break the monotony," then developing in intensity as it tells of the forward march, of trenches shelled all night, of moments when the voice was merged in the hissing of the shells until it could not be distinguished, and of times when the khaki-clad figures sat and stood at the post of duty expecting any time to be dashed into Eternity. Some of the lads have suffered death, and to-day several York homes will be cast into the vale of [illegible] mourning. Others have suffered wounds, but let the timorous recruit [illegible] hear of the cheerfulness of one of them, a York boy of 20, writing undaunted though taken into hospital [illegible]

BRIGHT AS A BEAUTIFUL SUNDAY MORNING.

His attitude is described in a letter from the Rev. J. [illegible], Wesleyan chaplain attached to the 1st [illegible] Field Ambulance, West Riding Division, in a note to Mr. and Mrs. W. Rutherford, 10, [illegible], Leeman-road, who are the parents of the lad, Private Stanley Rutherford, who joined the 5th West Yorks. in September last. Under date Sunday, May 9th, the chaplain writes:—"I have been having a talk with your son, who has been admitted to hospital slightly wounded. Let me say at once that there is no danger whatever attaching to his wounds, and it is only a matter of time before he will be quite well. At the present time he is able to walk about, and is as cheerful as any man I have seen for a long time. Altogether he has three wounds—one in each hand and one just below the shoulder. He received them about seven o'clock this (Sunday) morning. I am sure you have every reason to be proud of such a boy. He is a brave, manful fellow, and now that he is wounded is as bright as this beautiful Sunday morning. Let me assure you again that there is absolutely no cause for anxiety. He is well cared for, and the nature of his wounds is such that there is no fear at all of any permanent disablement."

The narrative which culminates in the engagement in which Private Rutherford was wounded commences by recounting how on the night of the 4th of May the men of the 5th West Yorks. set out from where they were billeted for the trenches, a distance of close on 10 miles, in full marching order in a pouring rain. Everyone was drenched to the skin, and in this condition they slept in the dug-outs on arrival, for in order to be ready for any surprise attack not an article of clothing or equipment has to be doffed. Approaching the trenches the Germans greeted the York boys with a hail of bullets and maxim gun fire, but no one was hit, although they had to march bent double in order to avoid it.

By Friday the regiment had only had a few casualties, two or three were wounded slightly, and one rather severely having been hit through the lungs by a sniper. On Friday night the enemy sent one or two shells over, but beyond blowing a few sandbags off an unoccupied length of the trenches they did no damage. The spirit in which the "Terriers" opposed the enemy at this stage is revealed in an excerpt from one of Sergt. Vollans' letters. "We all turn out and open fire on the Germans at 2.30 every morning, as this is the time they might try and break through our lines, as they are only 500 yards from us, but they'll get their jackets warmed if they start doing the dirt on the 5th."

A FIERCE BATTLE.

The jacket-warming process was soon to come, for on Saturday night, at 10.30, the order was given to stand to until about 12 midnight, during which time the Germans consistently shelled the trenches, but did very little damage to the portion occupied by "A" Company, and no one was hurt. On Sunday, however, a fierce battle took place. "The bombardment," says Vollans, "commenced at 5 a.m., and lasted along with rifle fire until 4.30 the next morning. Our troops were advancing on our left and right flanks, and the line our division was holding was in the centre. We got orders to hold these trenches at all cost. I was in charge of a section, being a section commander, and we opened a terrific fire on the enemy's position, but I am sorry to say my pal, who was in the next trench to me—only a wall made of sandbags—and another man between us, was shot through the head, and died soon afterwards, and we buried him the same evening. Birbeck, myself, and other two sergeants along with our two captains and the colonel, attended the funeral, the Colonel, of course, reading a short burial service over him. He was laid to rest along with other British heroes, about a mile from the firing line, in a small piece of ground selected for the purpose. He was a nice lad and lived in York. He had been my sleeping partner ever since we came out; in fact, he had always slept alongside of me ever since we were mobilised, so of course I miss him very much. He had only got engaged to be married whilst we were stationed at Gainsborough. He had breakfast with us the morning he was killed. I saw him fall, so to-day I am packing all his private and regimental kit up, the private kit for home. It makes one very bitter against them [illegible]

YORK MAN KILLED.

"The bombardment lasted all day with [illegible] shell fire, everybody expecting every minute would be their last, but [illegible] bravely; in fact, our adjutant told us he was proud to be with such a company [illegible]. We expect the Germans, whom we drove back, would make a counter-attack on us at night, but I think they must have lost more men than we did, as they never appeared. I had one or two narrow [illegible] myself, bullets whistling over my head and hitting sandbags used for cover [illegible] in front of me. On Monday morning at 4 o'clock I was ten yards from a poor fellow who had the top of his head blown off, one hand and his foot fearfully damaged. Of course he was killed instantly, another York fellow. I was the second one to his rescue, but of course all was over. Another of our fellows was blown to pieces on Sunday. My word, it isn't war but absolute murder. No picture can describe the scenes of yesterday, but thank God I have come through without a scratch so far. Two of the killed are Sergt. Batters and Private Wain. Monday was fairly quiet with the exception of previous to 4.30 a.m. when it was terrible. If I live to come back I shall have some things to talk about, if I had not much before. I feel sure we shall beat them, for dogged determination and pluck will do the job."

THE LEEDS RIFLES.

Another unit of the division, who, previous to going out to the front, were in training for some months at York, the Leeds Rifles, have fought with great gallantry and shown splendid steadiness under fire. Writing from the trenches a Leeds Rifleman records the death of Jack Tindall, the crack wing three-quarter, who played for Batley, and used to play for the Otley Rugby Union. If the news is true it will be received with universal regret by local footballers amongst whom he was idolised. He played in the charity match which took place a few months ago between the York Rugby Club and the Military, and contemplated giving his services to York for the season shortly before he received orders for the front. His training was with the 8th Battalion P.W.O. (Leeds Rifles), for whom he played prior to 1910. At the beginning of that season he joined the Otley Rugby Union Club, with whom he quickly rose to fame. As a wing three-quarter he had few peers. He was ubiquitous on the field, and once he got hold of the ball he was so fleet of foot that he could easily outdistance his pursuers. A rare pair were he and Hardwick, and with these two, along with Kenneth Duncan and Hiram Mason, both of whom are now in France, there was a line of offence and defence that was irresistible, and which culminated in winning the Yorkshire Challenge Cup for the second year in succession.

Tindall remained with the Otley club during the following season, 1911-12. An unfortunate incident in a match with Horton, on the old ground at Fagley, led to Tindall forsaking the Rugby Union. He was one of the most inoffensive of players. But at the Horton match he was sent off the field for striking—a clear mistake on the part of the referee. Being of a most sensitive disposition, Tindall never forgot the injury, and the following season he joined the Batley Northern Union club, with whom he was an even greater success than he had been with Otley. He was one of their most prolific scorers, and was regarded as such a star that he was the only player who was ever "billed" by Batley. "Jack Tindall is playing to-day" was announced whenever he was in the team.

Article in the Yorkshire Herald

The article then goes on to include a section about Private Rutherford who was wounded by three bullets to the shoulder on the Sunday 9th of May at the start of the battle.

A Fierce Battle

The jacket warming process was soon to come, for on Saturday night, at 10.30, the order was given to stand to until midnight during which time the Germans consistently shelled the trenches, but did little damage to the portion occupied by A Company, and no one was hurt. On Sunday however, a fierce battle took place: *'The bombardment', says Volans, 'commenced at 5 am and lasted along with rifle fire until 4.30 the next morning. Our troops were advancing on our left and right flanks and the line our division was holding was in the centre. We got orders to hold those trenches at all cost. I was in charge of a section, being a section commander, and we opened a terrific fire on the enemy's position, but I am sorry to say, my pal who was in the next trench to me – only a wall made of sandbags – and another man between us, was shot through the head and died soon afterwards and we buried him the same morning. Birbeck, myself, and another two sergeants along with our two captains and the colonel attending the funeral, with the colonel, of course, reading a short burial service over him. He was laid to rest with other British heroes about a mile from the firing line, in a small piece of ground selected for the purpose. He was a nice lad and lived in York. He had been my sleeping partner ever since we came out; in fact he had always slept alongside me ever since we had mobilised, so of course I miss him very much. He had only got engaged to be married whilst we were stationed at Sutton. He had breakfasted with us the morning he was killed. I saw him fall, so today I am packing all his private and regimental kit up, the private kit for home. It makes one very bitter against these dogs when a chum is put out of action, I can tell you.*

The bombardment lasted all day with terrific shell fire, everybody expecting every minute would be their last, but the lads bore it bravely; in fact our adjutant told us he was proud to be with such a courageous lot. We expect the Germans who we drove back, would make a counter attack on us at night; but I think they must have lost more men than we did, as they never appeared. I had one or two narrow squeaks myself, bullets whistling over my head and hitting sandbags used for cover just in front of me. On Monday morning at 4 o'clock I was ten yards from a poor fellow who had the top of his head blown off, one hand and his foot fearfully damaged. Of course he was killed instantly, another York fellow. I was the second one to his rescue, but of course all was over. Another of our fellows was blown to pieces on Sunday. (Walter Malthouse, his death is described by his sleeping partner Cpl A Wilson in '1915 The death of Innocence' by Lyn Mcdonald, the shell that killed him was British, falling short) My word, it isn't war but absolute murder. No picture can describe the scenes of yesterday, but thank God I have come through without a scratch so far. Two of the killed were Sargt. Batters and Private Wain. Monday was fairly quiet with the exception of previous to 4.30 am when it was terrible. If I live to come back I shall have some things to talk about, if I had not much before. I feel sure that we will beat them, for dogged determination and pluck will do the job.' This letter was written sometime between the evening of the 10th and the 12th.

On Monday 10th the Germans attacked the few Allied troops that had entered the German line and drove the remnants out closing up the line. This one-day assault had cost 458 officers and 11,000 men in casualties. Sir Douglas Haig was determined to carry on but his Divisional Generals could not bring together a coherent fighting force and they had no shells left for another assault. This fact caused uproar in parliament and the country.

On the 13th May, Charles received a bullet wound to his right thigh.

Aubers Ridge from the Allied side (Imperial War Museum)

The medical teams behind the lines, reported an extraordinary number of leg injuries during this engagement. The German machine guns seem to have been pre-set to sweep at leg level. The reason for this lies in the nature of the ground.

When the Guards Division held this line during the winter of 1915/16, they complained bitterly about the fact that they could not dig deep into the soil because the trenches would flood and could not be drained. Consequently, the trenches were built with a higher defensive parapet as Charles describes in his letter. Also there was no chance to dig communication trenches so that the troops had to move between the front line and support trenches overland. It would have been as Charles was moving back to support after the assault had stopped that he would have been hit by a pre-set machine gun firing across the top of the parapets trying to hit anyone exposed.

Army Form W3083 reveals that Charles was repatriated from No.18 General Hospital at Boulogne on 17th May on the Hospital Ship Andrew (below).

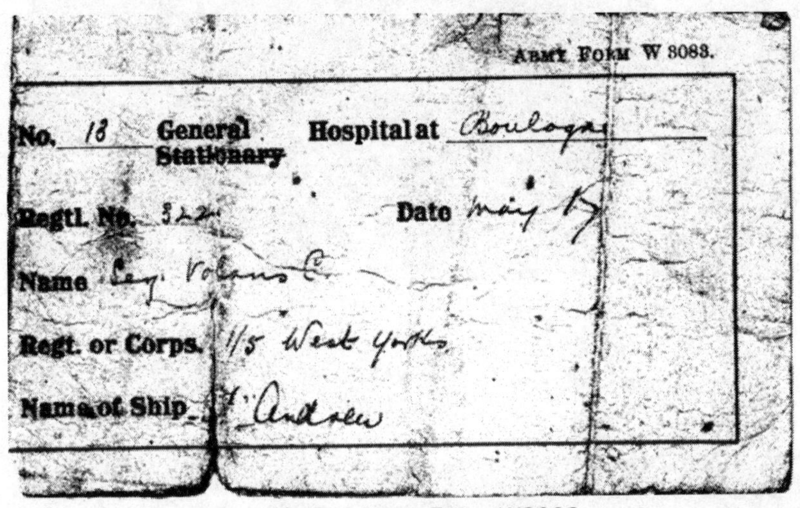

ARMY FORM W 3083.

No. 18 General ~~Stationary~~ Hospital at Boulogne

Regtl. No. 322[illegible] Date May 17

Name Sgt. Vollans C.

Regt. or Corps. 1/5 West Yorks

Name of Ship St. Andrew

Above: Army Form W3083
Below: Newspaper article

YORK TERRITORIAL WOUNDED.

CHEERY LETTER FROM SERGT. VOLLANS.

Sergt. Vollans, A Company, 1/5th West Yorkshire Regiment, whose stirring account of the York Territorials' share in the fighting around Ypres recently appeared in our columns, has since been wounded and is now in the London Military Hospital, Clifton-road, Lower Clapton, London, N.E. Sergt. Vollans is a son of Mr. and Mrs. Vollans, [illegible] and [illegible] Duncombe-place, York, and in a letter to his mother, dated May 19th, he states that on Thursday, May 13th, he had the misfortune to be hit by a German bullet which went through the thick part of the right thigh. Fortunately the bullet did not touch the bone. He was carried on a stretcher amidst a hail of bullets to the first aid dressing station, and after receiving attention was sent on to Boulogne, whence he crossed in a hospital ship to England. Sergt. Vollans states that he is receiving every attention in the London hospital, that his wound is mending splendidly, and that there is no need to worry; indeed, he expresses the hope that he will be sent home on sick furlough in a week or two.

Such a rapid return to England was routine for those with significant but not life threatening injuries. The mild injuries were treated at Main Dressing Stations and would then go to rest stations until they returned to their units. Severe injuries had initial life-saving surgery at the Casualty Clearing Stations before being sent to the Stationary Hospitals where more extensive work was done before repatriation.

Those who could wait were cleaned at the Dressing Stations and then passed quickly back through to the Base Hospitals from where they were evacuated to England leaving the beds nearer the front line ready for the more severe cases or the many that would not survive the transfer.

YORK SERGEANT AT THE FRONT.

Left and above: Newspaper photographs

Charles was in the City of London Military Hospital by the 20th May because he receives a telegram welcoming him home from Lillian Sonny Jarvis, one of the people who had sent him a telegram to wish him luck on leaving. Again his letter, written in reply to this telegram, was published in the newspaper along with two pictures of containing Charles, shortly after his discharge from hospital in June, again supporting the recruitment campaign.

'York Territorial Wounded, Cheery Letter from Sergt. Volans,

A Company, 1/5th West Yorkshire Regiment, whose stirring account of the York Territorials' share in the fighting around Ypres recently appeared in our columns, has since been wounded and is now in the London Military Hospital, Clifton Road, Lower Clapton, London NE. Sargt. Volans is a son of Mr. and Mrs.Volans, 4 and 5 Duncombe Place, York, and in a letter to his mother, dated May 19th, he states that on Thursday May 13th, he had the misfortune to be hit by a German bullet which went through the thick part of his thigh. Fortunately the bullet did not touch the bone. He was carried on a stretcher amidst a hail of bullets to the first aid dressing station, and after receiving attention was sent on to Boulogne whence he crossed in a hospital ship to England. Sargt. Volans states that he is receiving every attention in London hospital, that his wound is mending splendidly, and that there is no need to worry; indeed, he expresses the hope that he will be sent home on furlough in a week or two'.

After his discharge from Hospital in June 1915, he returned to York to the Regimental Barracks to recover and then start training the new recruits until in April 1916, Charles received his discharge from the army having served with the colours for 8 years; he was consequently considered time expired and became a civilian.

Herbert's Story

Because of their historical reputation as fighters, reinforced by their prowess in the first few months of the war, it was decided to bring all the Guards Regiments together to form a Guards Division.

The Division was formed in September 1915 under Major General the Earl of Cavan, a fighting leader popular with his men, who had commanded the 4th Guards

Brigade in fierce fighting through France from the start of the war. He was well renowned and had fought his brigade out of many difficult positions and was reputed with turning many apparent defeats into hard fought victories.

The Guards Division was made up of three Brigades, each of 4 Battalions of 1000 Guardsmen taken from the Coldstream, Grenadiers, Welsh, Irish and Scottish regiments.

So a Brigade, when fully staffed should have 4000 fighting Infantrymen and the Guards Division should have 12,000 Infantrymen when in the field.

Herbert's 3rd Battalion was in the 2nd Brigade under Brigadier-General J Ponsonby.

This Brigade was made up of 3rd Bttn. Grenadiers, 1st Bttn Coldstream, 1st Bttn Scots and 2nd Bttn Irish Guards plus a Machine Gun Company

The Guards Division was placed in 11th Corps under General Haking and were part of the First Army.

Herbert's Battalion comprised of 1007 men in total, with 30 Officers.

In the British Army, Companies are traditionally identified by letters, as were the territorial Battalions, except in the Guards, where they were described by numbers.

Each Company would have about 227 men and would be divided into 4 platoons of about 50 men, each having its own number and each with one or two officers in command.

Herbert was in 3 Company, 3rd Bttn Grenadier Guards. 3 Company contained 4 platoons, numbered 9,to 12. Herbert is in 9 platoon.

***

CHAPTER 6

HERBERT GOES TO FRANCE – THE BATTLE OF LOOS, OCTOBER 1915

At the end of July 1915, the 3rd Grenadiers were mobilised and transported to France via Southampton to Le Havre on the steamer, Queen Alexandra, protected by a Destroyer.

Herbert stayed with the Headquarters group in London until 4th October.

On arriving in Le Havre, the 3rd Battalion, under Col. NAL Curry DSO, entrained to Saint Omer in the Pas de Calais. They then marched on to billets in Esqueredes where they underwent 2 months of training learning the skills of bombing and how to use the new Lewis machine gun. On the 23rd August the 2nd Guards Brigade was formed.

On 25th September the Battalion marched to their base town of Vermelles arriving at 7 in the evening.

They spent the cold night trying to sleep in and around the remains of an old trench.

The next morning they moved south towards the village of Loos-en-Gohelle near the city of Lens in northern France, and entered the reserve trenches behind 1st Bttn Scots Guards.

Shortly after arriving in the support trenches they were tasked to support the 1st Scots along with the 2nd Irish Guards (in which Jack Kipling, the son of Rudyard Kipling, the writer, was a junior officer) and 1st Coldstream Guards, in an attack on a heavily defended German stronghold in a large colliery called Puits 14.

The attack started at 4pm and the platoons were sent straight out into No-man's land as they reached the front line. It was during this attack that Jack Kipling (the son of

Rudyard Kipling the writer) was seen to take a bullet in the neck and fall. Because of the intensity of the firing it was not possible to bring him back to the lines and medical support. He was never seen again and despite years of work by his parents, his grave was not identified until 1992 and confirmed in 2010.

Although the leading troops managed to get into the German front line, they were driven out by machine guns firing from strong defensive positions that had been prepared by the Germans for almost a year.

The Grenadiers withdrew and fell back to support the Coldstream guards who had dug into a chalk pit to the left of the Grenadier's and Scots' line. Here they reinforced and held the British line to Loos until they were taken out of the line on the night of the 30th.

This battle was one of the early, organised attempts to break through the German lines. The Corps' commanders had discovered at Aubers ridge that assaulting the deep trench lines was difficult and new tactics were being tried in this assault.

The concept of the co-ordination of artillery, air cover and ground troops was yet to be invented. Once a battle started, communication between the various forces and the HQ was very primitive, based on easily broken telephone lines and easily injured human messengers.

The Battalion was allowed to rest in billets until 4th October when it returned to trenches outside Vermelles opposite the Hohenzollen Redoubt, a complex of German trenches only yards away from the British lines.

On the 8th, the Battalion was subject to a surprise attack by the Germans driving the 2nd and 3rd Companies out of their trenches until with support from bombers sent from the 3rd Battalion Coldstream Guards who were on their right in the line, the Guards drove the attack back out of their trenches during which 2nd Lt. Agar Roberts of 3 Company was wounded.

On the 10th October the Battalion was withdrawn to billets in Vermelles.

On the 9th, Herbert, as part of a reinforcing detail of officers and men, arrived in the rear area near Vaudricourt where they were held in reserve until the 15th.

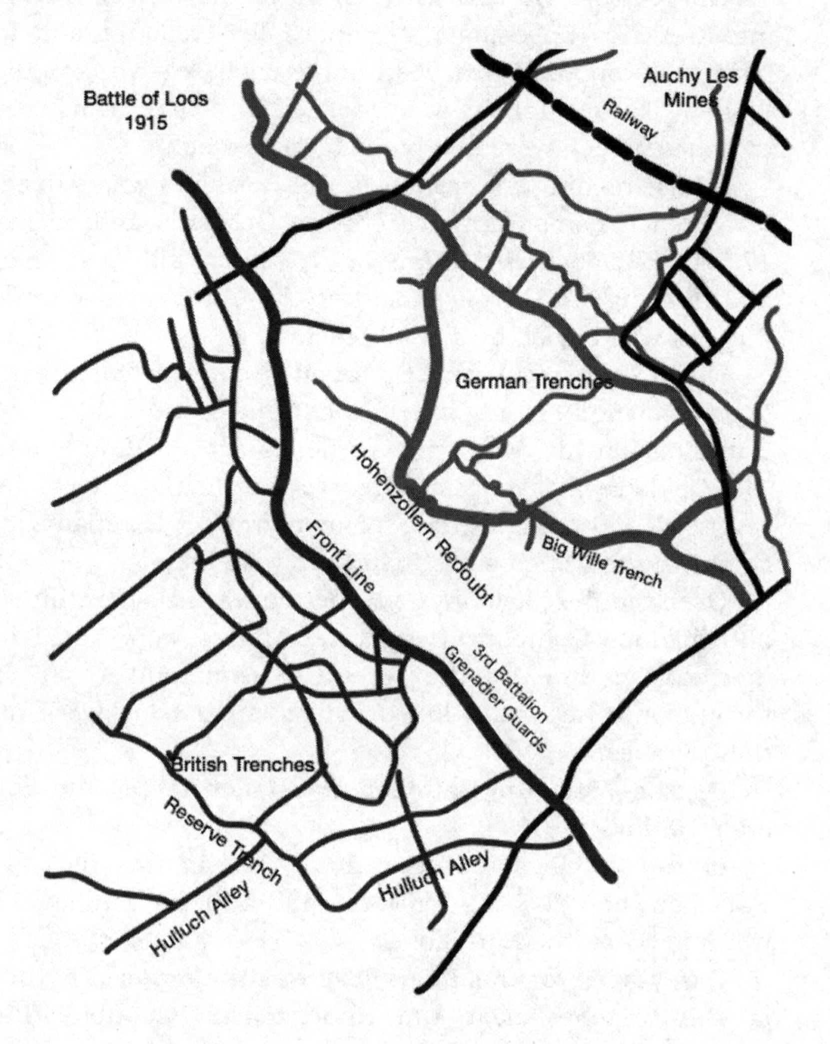

Hohenzollern

The 'Battle of Loos' had officially ceased. The attempts to advance into German territory were halted and the frontline was consolidated. It was during this period that the mobile war changed into the siege warfare that is the hallmark of the First World War.

On the 15th Herbert with his Battalion were sent back into trenches opposing the Hohenzollen redoubt and in particular opposite the German trench known as 'Big Willie'. The Battalion was tasked with improving the trenches, which were in a badly damaged state.

Whilst holding the trenches, the Battalion was subject to a steady bombardment from the Germans and on the 17th there was a particularly heavy attack, killing 11 men and injuring 32. During this attack, 4 Company's officers' dug out was buried by a shell blast.

During the night, the Battalion second in command, Major Molyneux-Montgomerie, went out to the right of the Battalion, on his own, with a rifle, to try and find where the Coldstream Guards were. Having found them, he returned and took a group of men from 3 Company, to complete the trench so as to link up with them.

Over the next few days the German attacks continued and all four Company Sergeant - Majors were killed or injured. On the 21st the second in command was shot through the head and killed whilst supervising work on the trenches.

On the 25th, the Battalion was taken out of the line after 10 days.

In the 20 days that they had been in the line, the Battalion had lost 19 officers and 500 men killed or wounded; half the Battalion.

One reason for this heavy loss was the exposed nature of the trenches near the Hohenzollen Redoubt. This German stronghold was close to the British lines and looking down on them.

Another was that the Battalion had to learn how to operate in this dangerous war zone; the Loos battle was their first exposure to the trenches. The Officers had their handbooks on how best to organise their troops and defences, but these were based on pre-1914 experiences. A new manual on trench warfare did not come out until March 1916 and of course reading a book is a world away from actually doing the job on the ground.

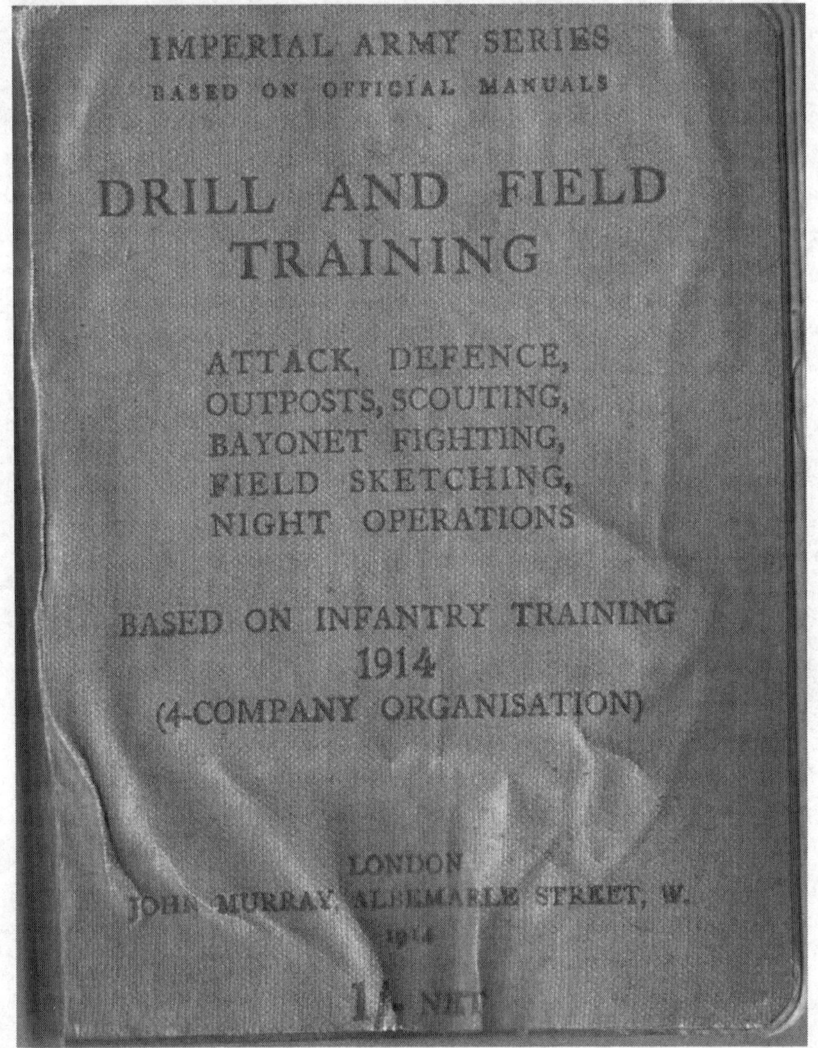

On the 25th October, the Battalion marched to Bethune where they boarded a train taking them west to the town of Lillers from where they marched into billets at the village of Norentes Fontes. Over the next few days new officers arrived to replace the fallen, including Lt. Raymond Asquith, the prime minister's son.

In the Trenches near Neuve Chappelle: Winter 1915

On the 8th November the Battalion marched north east, 26 km, to La Gorgue near the HQ town of Estaires staying in new billets until the 14th when they marched to trenches just north of Neuve Chappelle (The same area Charles Volans had been fighting in May 1915).

This area was considered a quiet section but the trenches were knee deep in water. The troops complained that they would prefer shelling to the discomfort of the constant water.

Because the conditions were so bad, the troops rotated every 2 days between the rear billets and the trenches.

On the 2nd of December the Battalion re-entered the trenches near Neuve Chappelle, between Sion Post lane and Moated Grange North. Although the area was considered quiet, to enter the trenches because of the water levels, the men still had to go above ground exposed to enemy fire instead of entering via communication trenches as was becoming normal practice as the war progressed.

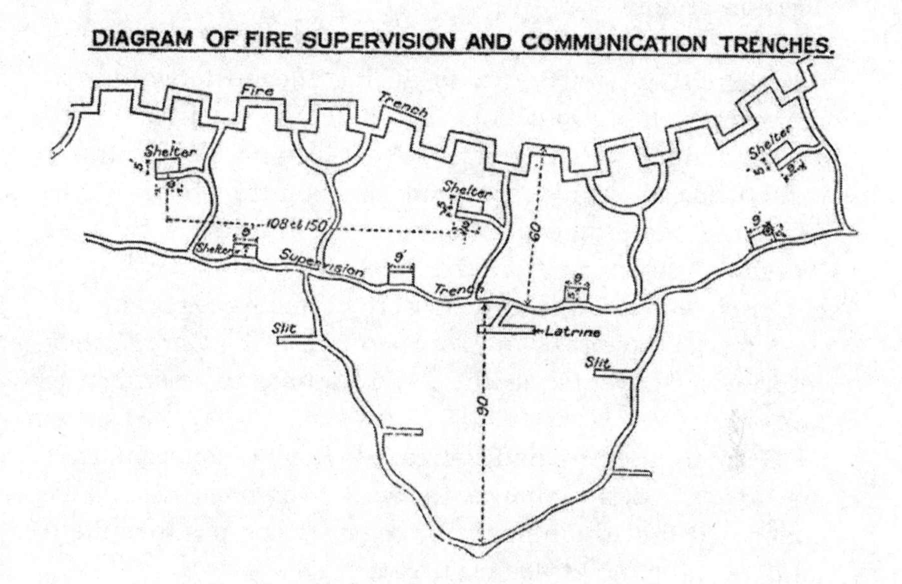

During the night, patrols explored the shell holes in no-man's land whilst the rest of the Battalion spent time improving the trenches, in particular building drainage systems to keep the water levels down.

The Germans seemed particularly quiet and there were very few casualties until a new German artillery commander arrived on the 24th and organised a severe and accurate artillery assault on the British trenches.

On the 25th the Battalion was in the trenches and the men celebrated Christmas with plum pudding and a pint of beer each, before withdrawing from the trenches on Boxing Day and marching to Merville for a short rest period.

1916

As the first day of 1916 opened, the Battalion was on the move again, marching north to Laventie between Loos and Ypres, taking over the billets of the Scots Guards before relieving them in the Line to the left of the Guards Division sector.

Since the trenches here were in good condition, the Battalion spent its free time during the next two weeks improving the protection by building splinter proof shelters since the Germans were keeping up a steady bombardment of the rear communication trenches.

At the same time the Guards were training a troop of Wiltshire Yeomanry, from the New Army, in the principles of trench warfare. The guards were becoming experts.

After 10 days rest and recuperation at La Gorgue they returned to Laventie on the 24th January to re-enter the line.

German shelling had increased, raising concerns that an attack was imminent, and everyone was very concerned that there might be a gas attack but, despite a lot of shelling, no attack occurred.

On February 1st the Battalion moved to Merville again for 7 days rest before returning to the trenches at Riez Bailleul until the 16th. Trench life continued as usual with patrols going out into No-man's land during the night. Otherwise there was little to gossip about, although a lieutenant in 2 Company fell into the trench on returning from a patrol in the early morning and got a British bayonet through his lower leg.

After the 16th February, the Battalion moved back in stages towards Calais, arriving there on the 5th March and staying in Camp Beaumarais for two weeks for training with the new hand grenades that were replacing the handmade bombs that the troops had been making for themselves out of jam tins and cordite, up to this time.

During training, 4 Company had an accident; a premature explosion on throwing the bomb resulted in 5 killed and 16 wounded including the officer in charge of the party.

On the 16th March the Battalion started moving towards Ypres, entering the support trenches in the salient on the 26th.

***

CHAPTER 7

YPRES 1916

Ypres today from Sanctuary wood

The City of Ypres had been at the centre of a salient sticking into the German Line since the formation of the Western Front in December 1914. The British forces had been centered on this city since the start of the war.

The City was on a plain surrounded on three sides by low hills held by the Germans.

From their positions, the Germans were able to see the allied troops moving across the plain and consequently shelled all the main routes up to the allied lines as well as the city itself, which was now in ruins. As well as shelling, the city was also subject to gas attacks whenever the wind was in a favourable direction for the Germans.

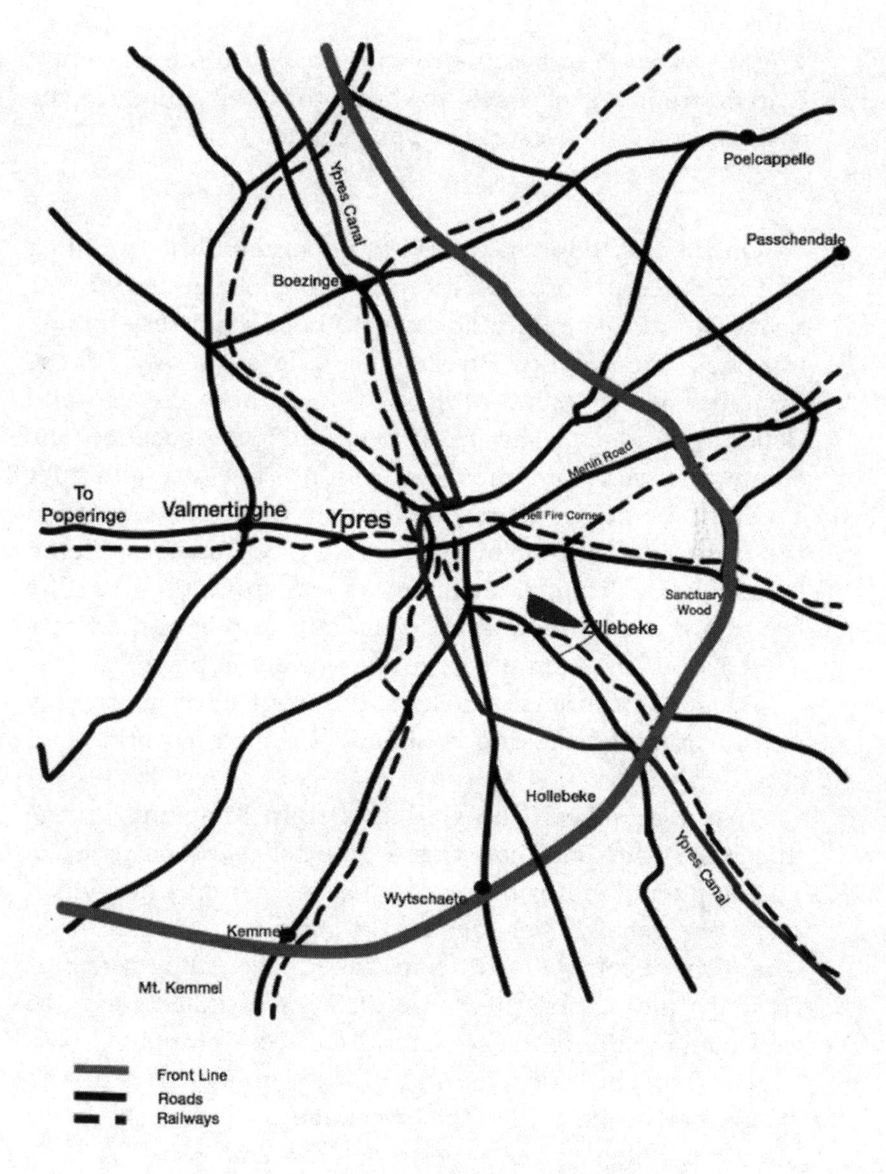

Ypres

Despite the state of ruin in the city, it was still used by the troops for short periods of rest. There was a well known coffee shop in the ruins of the Grand Place called 'Old Tom's' where the troops could get a hot drink whilst waiting to move out of the town, either into the warren of British trenches or back towards the civilisation of the rest camps to the west, near Poperinghe.

On the 30th March, the Battalion entered the front line in the Eastern Ypres sector near Zillebeke, relieving the Scots Guards. The Battalion was to hold some very broken trenches from Duke Street to Roulers railway. These trenches were swept with fire from the Pilkem and Belleward ridges. The relief was difficult because the communication trenches and front line were under constant bombardment. 1, 3 and 4 Companies reached the front line without injury but No. 2 Company suffered heavily from shrapnel shells on its way up to the line. The fire and the mud made it very difficult to relieve the Scots Guards, but by 4 am the Grenadiers were in place.

Because of intense shelling, the front line was rapidly cut off from HQ making it difficult to make reports or to receive orders.

To try and keep the Germans from attacking during this relief, the Battalion was supported by 3 batteries of 18 pounder guns firing on the German front line, which made the relief easier for the Battalion than it had been when the Scots Guards had taken over the trenches. During this effort there were 5 men killed and 16 wounded including the commander of 1st Company.

The Trenches were found to be severely damaged, and troops had to lie under the wreckage to find shelter, but they were able to defend the trench system.

Over the next few days the troops slowly improved the trenches, trying to get the water to drain away, which they found it would not do, despite there being a slope away from the trenches. All the wooden revetments were destroyed and there was standing water in every shell hole, however the troops managed to 'improve' things to such an extent that they were able to crawl along the trench without exposing themselves.

On April 3rd the Battalion withdrew to a camp just west of Vlamertinghe, for 4 days rest before returning to their old trenches and found them destroyed again after a heavy bombardment whilst they were being held by the Scots Guards.

For the next 4 days the Germans seemed to have exhausted themselves on the Scots so life was again quieter and nothing much seemed to happen.

For the rest of April and May, the Battalion rotated between rest areas near Poperinghe, where 4 soldiers were killed and 2 injured when German artillery fired on them whilst they were unloading officers kit, and either the frontline or support trenches. During this period, the Guards were issued with steel helmets for the first time.

Some trenches were better preserved than others but all were very wet. The standing water could not be drained and any movement during the day drew fire so all work had to be done at night. There were casualties every day.

Night Patrols reported a lot of activity in the German lines, whilst the Battalion spent a lot of time draining the trenches, putting out wire and repairing the parapet to improve protection or re-digging trenches that had been destroyed by shell fire.

When stationed in the support lines in Ypres, they supplied nightly fatigue parties, carrying wood for the mining parties digging towards the Messines ridge, and putting wire in front of the support trenches.

Out of Ypres

On the 1st June the whole 2nd Guards Brigade moved to a training area near Volckerinckhove across the border in France, to the west of Poperinghe, well behind the lines, where they practiced new methods of attack in a reproduction of the German lines built by the Corps' Engineers.

The new tactics involved attacking in 5 waves. The first two Companies advanced in 2 waves about 50 yards apart. These waves were intended to cross the German first and second line trenches without entering them and pass on to the German third line, which they were intended to take.

The third wave was planned to pass over the German front line and take the second line. The fourth wave was to take the German front line.

Each Company has bombing parties on each flank whose job is to block the German communication trenches. The first waves were to establish blocks to control access to the attackers and the following waves of bombers should help clear the communication trenches.

Each man had to carry 2 bombs and 4 sandbags and every third man had to carry a shovel.

The 5th wave was from another Battalion and was tasked with carrying up supplies for the advancing troops.

At night the soldiers had to carry Roman candles to show the position of the waves.

The Battalions practiced until they had mastered the exercise and then the Brigade practiced en masse.

This training confirmed to the troops that there was going to be 'a Big Push' and they were going to be involved.

On the 14th of June the Battalion was moved by lorry to Vlamertinghe and returned to the Ypres salient, their task being to replace the 9th Canadian Battalion who had suffered heavy losses occupying the trenches at the west end of Zillbeke Lake.

After 4 days the Battalion moved on to the recently retaken trenches at Sanctuary Wood replacing the 1st Bttn. Scots Guards. They found them in bad condition covered with fallen trees and wire left behind by the Germans who had been holding them.

Patrols into No-man's land found that the Germans had pulled out of their old trenches, leaving dead bodies, equipment and ammunition. Over 350 rifles were salvaged by the troops.

Top: Sanctuary wood 1919
Bottom: Sanctuary wood now

On the 19th and 20th they suffered a heavy bombardment resulting in many casualties leaving the troops desperate for their relief from the trenches. At last they withdrew to the camps behind Ypres, to rest for a week.

After this period in the line, they moved to a reserve area near the Yser Canal until the 30th when they returned to the front line. During the next three days there was a lot of artillery activity on both sides. The Welsh Guards were preparing for an assault and the Germans responded by shelling the communication trenches to prevent the troops coming forward.

To protect their troops during this bombardment, 3rd Battalion withdrew troops from the front line, into saps off the communication trenches, and as a consequence there were few casualties.

Over the next three weeks, the Battalion rotated between the support line on the canal bank and the front line before leaving the Ypres area on the 25th and heading south.

By the 31st July, the Battalion had reached Le Souich near Amiens in the northern Somme region where they acted as labour to help with trench digging for other Battalions.

On the 9th August the Battalion had an 'informal' visit from the King. The soldiers would have been cleaning and polishing their kit and uniforms for days before the King arrived although there was no formal inspection or parade. They then entered the trenches around Albert, alternating with training camps near Sailly-au-Bois, before they moved towards their assembly area near Morlancourt.

***

CHAPTER 8

THE SOMME

July to November 1916

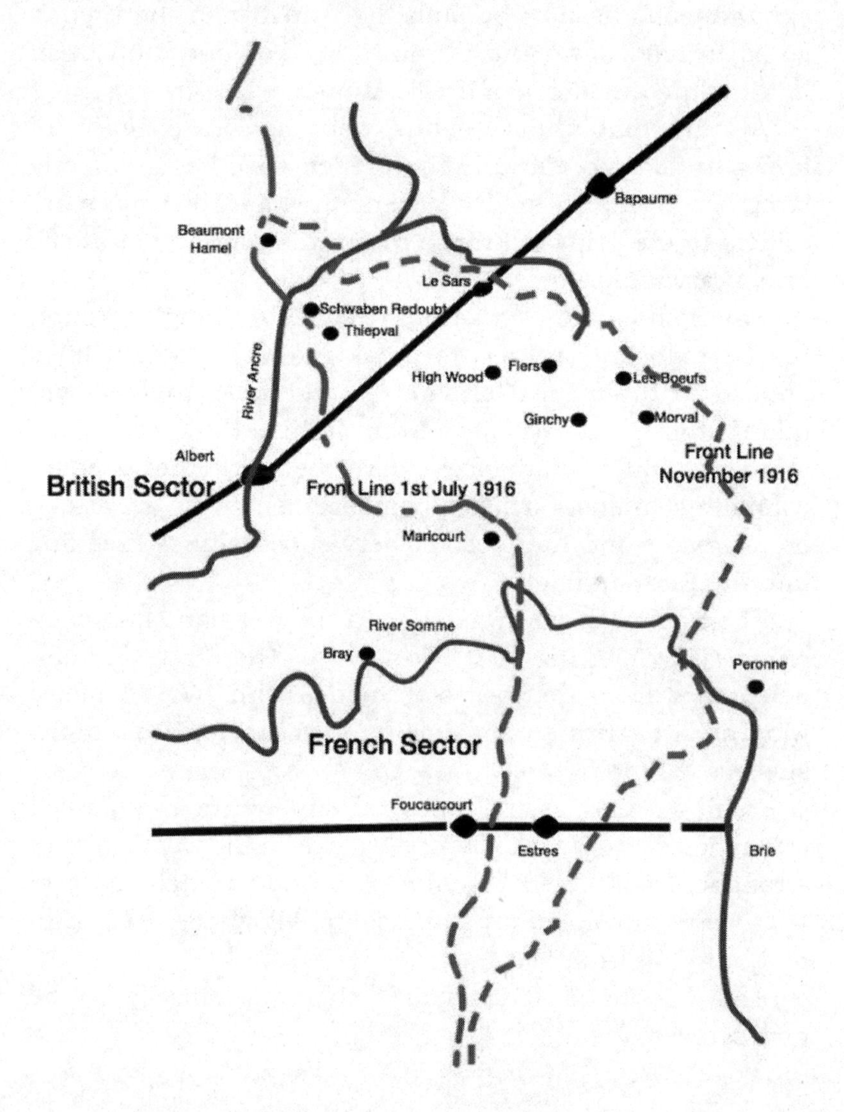

The Somme Battlefield

For the last 2 years the Allied forces had been fighting local battles along the line of trenches and had been unable to break through the German defences because the Germans could bring reinforcements in from the lines on either side to block any advance.

Consequently it was decided that there should be a simultaneous assault by both the British and the French so as to hold down the German reserves and stop them moving into any areas of breakthrough.

At this time the Germans were heavily engaged in trying to take Verdun and the French were being severely stretched trying to hold a salient that had become more critical to the pride of France rather than for any strategic or military importance.

The Somme attack was not designed to break through the German line, rather, to break into the German lines and so to draw the Germans in and wear them down, taking the pressure off Verdun. This 'Bite and Hold' strategy, which had been developed by the French, combining intense artillery bombardment with an attack on a broad front, had become very successful at breaking into the German line.

The Somme region was an area the Germans had been reinforcing for the last two years. The first German defences were a network of trenches with two 40 metre wide belts of wire entanglements in front, and reinforced shelters behind.

Behind the front lines, there were reinforced strongholds built into every village and wood. Every stronghold contained machine guns and trench mortars and were connected by tunnels to allow the troops to move around under cover.

The Germans considered their defences to be impregnable.

The first assault started on the 1st July, with both the northern sector and southern sector driven into, taking several villages but costing thousands of lives of the British forces. The assault continued until the 14th by which date, a 3 mile section of the second line of trenches had been taken, but at an enormous cost in men.

The 49th West Riding Division was involved in this phase of the battle against the German stronghold, the Schwaben Redoubt, on Thiepval Ridge. This was one of the hardest fought areas and the casualty list was horrific.

On 28th July 1916 Charles re-enlisted with a new number of 202432 and got recruitment, home leave pass from the Colliergate Barracks until 1st August.

For the next few weeks whilst attached to the reserve Battalion 3/5th West Yorkshires he tried to acquire a commission, getting references from his old headmaster and one of his senior officers, Lt. Col. CS Lorri, who was awaiting a medical board report before he was allowed to return to the Division. Charles wished to join the Army Service Corps, the logistics service that was needed to keep the division in the field. His attempts to gain a commission seem to have failed and he returned as Company Sgt. Major in the ASC working as an Audit Clerk on a salary of 4 shillings a day increasing to 5 shillings when he went out to the front.

The second phase of the Somme attack started on July 18th and culminated on September 9th with an advance that ended with the 16th Irish Division taking the village of Ginchy. They were then reinforced by 2nd Grenadiers, who forced the last Germans out of the orchard at the north eastern corner of the village during the night of the 13th/14th September. After this advance the attacking troops were sitting in a salient with the German held towns of Morval on the right and Thiepval on the left.

The third phase was to drive into these areas with the British taking Morval and the French driving into Combles towards Thiepval.

The Guards were now brought in to lead the assault. This was the assault that the 2nd Brigade, including Herbert's Battalion, had been practicing for during June whilst on 'rest periods' from holding the line in the Ypres Salient.

The second Guards Brigade was to fight on the right with the 1st Brigade on the left and the 3rd Brigade as reserve.

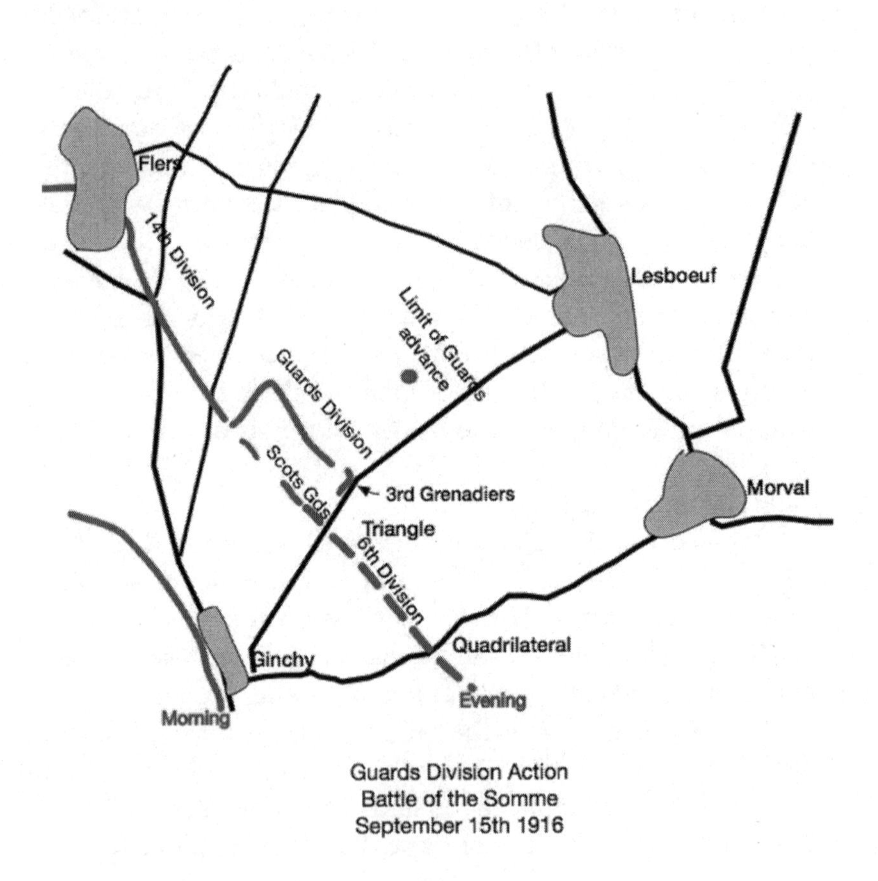

Guards Division Action
Battle of the Somme
September 15th 1916

Their instructions were to attack the enemy defences between Combles and Martinpuich and to seize the villages of Morval, Les Boeufs, Gueudencourt and Flers.

Herbert, as usual, was in 3rd Company, led by Captain Hopley, supported by Lt. Champneys, 2nd Lt.Worsley and 2nd Lt. Cornish.

On the 12th of September they entered the support line.

On the 14th the Battalion sent back their packs and greatcoats along with their surplus kit, leaving them with just their fighting kit. They were issued with bombs and sandbags, tools and took up position at 9 pm.

The Battalion was to assault in columns of half Companies with 50 yards between each platoon. Number 3 Company was on the right with 10 platoon marching on the left and 9 platoon on the right. Behind them were 12 platoon on the left and 11 platoon on the right.

The 3rd Battalion was on the right of the line with the 1st 2nd and 3rd Battalions of Coldstream Guards on the left around the village of Ginchy. The 6th Division was on their right, with the 71st Brigade consisting of the 1st Leicesters, on the immediate right of 3 Company, with the 9th Norfolk Regiment on their right.

As the troops had advanced to their assembly points they had heard engines being serviced and tested and had seen large lozenge shaped machines covered in tarpaulins and camouflage nets. These were being called tanks and were alleged to be for carrying water!

At 2 am, the troops were quietly taking their places when three of these tanks with the letters A, B and C painted on their sides, ground to a halt within the village of Ginchy between the 3rd Grenadiers and the 1st Coldstream. Three young officers, Lt. Tull, 2nd Lt. Clarke and 2nd Lt. Smith climbed out and introduced themselves to the Guards senior officers to get a briefing about the battlefield in front of them.

Tanks on the Somme, September 1916
(Imperial War Museum)

At 4 am the troops were in position behind the village of Ginchy, about 100 yards behind the front line and their start points. Here they were issued sandwiches and rum and tried to get some sleep.

At 5.40 the Troops had reached their start points and the tank engines were started and they set out through the mist, into No-man's land along the Ginchy to Les Boeufs road. Immediately after starting, Tank A commanded by Lt. Tully, broke its tail wheels and turned back leaving B and C to carry on without it. Tanks B and C moved randomly into the battlefield, bouncing in and out of trenches and shell holes that threatened to engulf the tanks. Although the tank commanders had compasses to guide them, these were found to be useless because of the violent motion of the tank and the fact that the tank was made of steel made the compasses spin! Lt's Clarke and Smith had never been in a battle zone before, their practice areas had been flat even ground; the crews were thrown around in their machines as they tried to drive forward. As they advanced they came under rifle fire from defending troops in forward positions. By luck they were on target and passed up their lane of wire. Clarke in B tank had reached the German front line and turned left, (north) up Straight trench firing on the German troops with his machine guns. Smith probably pushed straight on beyond the German front line.

At 6.15 the order came to fix bayonets and at 6.20 the order to attack.

On the map, it looked simple. When the whistles blew the troops would rise out of the trenches and walk in single file towards the Les Boeufs road and church about 600 yards ahead.

The ground around Ginchy had been under artillery bombardment since the start of the offensive in July and was a mass of shell holes and irregular ridges of churned soil stretching into the early morning mist.

There were no landmarks in any direction and the wire and metal shells in the soil made compasses spin uselessly when the officers tried to guide their troops.

The troops were in a great desert of shell holes with their own barrage in front of them and the German barrage behind them.

To make things difficult, there was a lane of uncut wire left for the tanks to run along, between the right and left columns of the attack and also on the right of the Battalion.

As the attack started, a creeping barrage moved forward at 50 yards per minute with the troops following as closely as possible to catch the Germans as they came out of their deep cover. In response, the Germans pounded the village of Ginchy where they thought the British troops were, leaving the attacking troops between the two fire storms.

As the line advanced the Coldstream Guards drifted to the left leaving a gap between the 3rd Bttn. Coldstream and the 3rd Bttn. Grenadiers which maintained their straight line. This gap was filled by the 2nd Battn. Grenadiers, who were coming forward in support.

Soon after starting, the Guards came on some unexpected lines made of loosely connected shell holes manned by the Germans. These were the troops who had fired on the tanks as they went by. Because they were not known to be there, they had not been specifically targeted by the artillery during the initial bombardment and the creeping barrage had passed them too quickly to do much harm.

The Guards were not in a mood to take prisoners and all the Germans were shot or bayoneted. This unexpected resistance resulted in minor delays so that the following Companies caught up with the leading troops. In these shell holes, 2nd Lt. Worsley from 3rd Company was injured leading a combined assault on the German defences.

Because of these holdups, the whole brigade became mixed with different Battalions in the same place so they advanced as a brigade en masse.

Wherever the leading Companies were held up, the following troops would come up and assist, trying to get around the side of any stronghold.

On the left, 4 Company were particularly hard hit with the commander Captain Mackenzie receiving a mortal wound. However he got up and struggled on until hit again. Even then he got up onto one knee to cheer 4 Company on before collapsing. He was later carried out of the battlefield alive but died whilst being taken towards the rear aid station. Lt. Asquith (the Prime Minister's son) fell in the same place as he led groups of 4 Company.

On the Battalion's right was the complex of German strongholds called the Quadrilateral. This was the objective for the 6th Division and was due to be attacked and rolled over by the tanks deployed in their support.

Top: War artist's impression of the evening after the attack
Below: Photo: View of site of Straight trench looking towards the Quadrilateral

The main mass attack was making rapid progress but the right flank, with Herbert, was suffering from the fire from the Quadrilateral. 2nd Lt. Cornish led 3 Company and parts of 1 Company in a push towards the right getting within 200 yards of the German fortifications where they set up heavy covering fire that drove the German defenders into cover and suppressed their fire. As they looked over towards the Quadrilateral, there was the shape of a single tank driving slowly along the front of the German defences.

The main assault entered their first objectives, Straight Trench; were they found the Germans were very keen to surrender, perhaps after the shock of being assaulted by a tank, unlike the soldiers in the intermediate trenches who had fought to the death. Shortly after reaching the objective, the tank turned back to the British lines, possibly because the Guards commanders felt it was drawing fire on itself putting the attack troops at risk.

On reaching the objective the men were out of breath so rested whilst they grouped prisoners together before sending them back towards the British lines. As the prisoners went back they were machine gunned by their own guns, but most ran and got to the British lines.

No 1 Company was holding the right flank and was attempting to contact the 1st Leicesters of 6th Division. They could see into the German trenches towards the Quadrilateral and fired down them at the machine guns that 3 Company were engaging.

Because the Coldstream Guards and 1st Irish Guards had drifted to the left and the 1st Scots Guards had followed 3rd Battalion, there was a gap between the two groups. The Adjutant, Capt. Lyttleton, of 3rd Battalion took 100 men to try to find the Coldstream Guards and became detached and fell in with the Coldstream and Irish Guards. When this group reached their objectives, they realised that the trenches to the right were still occupied by the Germans.

Their commanding officer obviously had to organise to clear this area and Capt. Lyttleton took a party of Irish Guards and bombed their way down the trenches to be met by Germans running the other way being chased by the 2nd Battalion Grenadiers from the 1st Brigade who had forced forwards and had filled the space between the two attacking columns.

The whole of the first objective was now held and the advance on the second objective was planned.

Photo: Taken on the Somme, carrying a wounded soldier from the field (Not Herbert or Lt. Cornish.) (Courtesy Imperial War Museum)

On the extreme right the advance was still blocked because of the Quadrilateral stronghold. 3 Company, under Lt. Cornish kept up a heavy enfilade fire onto the Germans in the Quadrilateral. The returning fire hit Lt. Cornish. Herbert who was fighting with his officer picked him up, throwing him across his shoulders and carried him back towards the village to an aid post. With his lieutenant on his shoulders and bending forward to carry the weight, he was hit in his buttock by a German bullet. Despite his wound, he managed to carry his officer back to the regimental aid post at Ginchy.

Further towards the left, the Battalion made progress although when they reached their supposed second objective, they were really only half way between the first and second objectives when the Royal Flying Corps photographs were studied.

The commanders could see into Les Boeufs and they could see the Germans pulling back towards Bapaume taking their heavy guns with them.

Les Boeufs now, from the point of the Guards' furthest advance.

At this point, the German Line had been broken. There was a way through to open country. The bloody attrition of the last 10 weeks seemed to have paid off.

Captain Lyttleton again took a mixed group of 120 troops from the Irish and Grenadier Guards and pushed on another 800 yards coming to a field of standing crops. Here they recognised that they were very exposed and held the position whilst sending runners back to Brigade HQ for reinforcements to consolidate the position and take advantage of the breakthrough.

Because of the terrible state of the ground, the difficulty in communication, and the lack of understanding of the situation back at HQ, the reinforcements did not come forward and by 1pm the Germans were infiltrating back into their lines.

By 6pm Capt. Lyttleton and his advance party was surrounded by Germans.

The group decided to fight their way out and retreat to their new front line.

As he had run out of ammunition Captain Lyttleton threw his revolver at group of Germans. They thought it was a mills bomb and dived away letting the remains of the advance party break out and run back towards the British front line where they turned and held off the Germans, who, realising they had been tricked, followed the retreating Guardsmen.

The 2nd Guards Brigade was pulled out of the battle on the 16th September, and was replaced by the 61st Infantry Brigade.

The 3rd Battalion had suffered enormous casualties. Of 22 officers who went into action 17 had been killed or wounded including the Battalion commander. 7 had been killed outright including Raymond Asquith, 2 were mortally wounded and died whilst passing back through the hospital system. 8 more were wounded. 395 men from the ranks, including Herbert, were killed or wounded.

After handing over Lt. Cornish to the medical team at the Regimental Aid post, a sheltered area, probably in a ruined cellar or large shell hole just behind the start trench, Herbert would have passed back through the lines.

Advanced Dressing Station (Courtesy Imperial War Museum)

At the aid post, he would have had a bandage applied and morphine given if he needed it. If he could walk, he would have been directed towards the Advanced Dressing Station (ADS) in the support area, maybe helped by a stretcher bearer, who would also be one of the Regimental band when the Battalion was not under fire.

The ADS was larger and sometimes more protected. Here, simple treatments could be applied, and the first wheeled patient transport would be available for stretcher cases. Anyone needing more than a simple dressing would be sent on to the Casualty Clearing station which was placed behind the heavy artillery emplacements.

Typical Casualty Clearing Station - 1916

Here there was a large Reception tent capable of holding 20 patients, where the orderlies would cut away the uniforms and clean the wounds to expose the damage.

Those needing resuscitation would be placed in the Resuscitation tent where they would get to lie in a warm bed and might get a fresh blood transfusion direct from a mate, if necessary. From there they pass to the Pre-op tent and then into the Operation tent where there would be 6 tables working with 3 surgeons moving between the tables as they were loaded.

Here the wounds were cleaned and all damaged tissue cut out to prevent gangrene and sepsis. After dressings by the orderlies, the patient was moved to the Evacuation tent to await the ambulance convoy, or if they were either too bad for evacuation or only had a minor wound and could return to the line, they would go to the ward tent where they could be watched for 24 hours. Those too bad for further evacuation would be cared for whilst they died, receiving morphine or cigarettes to comfort them.

Many of the graveyards on the battlefields today, are at the sites of Casualty Clearing Stations.

Like Charles the previous year, Herbert passed quickly through to the Base Hospital close to Calais or Le Havre. Herbert arrived in England on the 19th September only 3 days after his injury, staying in the UK until the 18th January 1917.

For their actions, Lt. Cornish was awarded the Military Cross for the attack on the Quadrilateral and Herbert was awarded the Military medal for his rescue.

Back at the Somme, eventually all the objectives were taken. The pressure on Verdun was relieved and a relatively large area of territory was taken.

Within 6 months of this assault, the Germans had withdrawn from their trenches back towards a deep defensive line, the Hindenburg line.

After his wounds had healed in hospital, Herbert would have been given a short period of leave when he would have gone home to Thirsk, before returning to the Guards depot at Caterham, known to the troops as 'Tin Town'.

At Caterham, Herbert joined the Reserve Battalion. This had been formed in 1914 to retrain the troops who had come back to the colours at the outbreak of war. By 1916, there were 4 Companies of new troops in training, a fifth Company of troops on special duties and 4 Companies (labelled 6 to 9) made up of troops returning to France after recovery from injury.

1917 in the trenches: Albert region

Herbert returned to France on the 19th January, and rejoined his Battalion when they came out of the trenches on the 24th January into billets in Mericourt. During February they spent a lot of time training in the area. On the 9th February, whilst practicing with mills bombs, a bomb went off without leaving the muzzle of its launching rifle injuring an officer and three men whilst the rest of the Companies were watching.

On the 26th they marched to Maurepas near Albert, and entered the front line for 5 days sending out patrols to test the wire and the German defences.

On the 8th March after 3 days rest in Maurepas, they moved back into the trenches where they found it very quiet because the Germans were withdrawing into the fortified complex, the 'Hindenberg' line stretching from Lens to Soissons.

On the 16th March, the Battalion advanced after the Germans through St. Pierre Vaast Wood and into Vaux Wood.

On the 18th they were relieved and sent back to supply labour, building a railway designed to bring supplies up from the major railhead to the support areas of the trenches.

During April and May the Battalion split in two and alternated a mixture of fatigues, road making and loading trucks behind the lines, with training in the Clery region.

On the 17th of June they re-entered the line relieving the 1st Bttn Scots Guards acting as support around the HQ at Bluet Farm. After the quiet of the last few weeks, there was a steady increase in shelling and a steady trickle of casualties. For the first time, the troops were bothered by enemy aircraft and were under orders to keep under cover during daylight.

On the 26th a shell fell on 3 Company's bomb store, just as the new junior officer, 2nd Lt. Dunlop, stepped out of it, having spent all day in the store. The men left inside were killed.

Charles Returns to the Front:

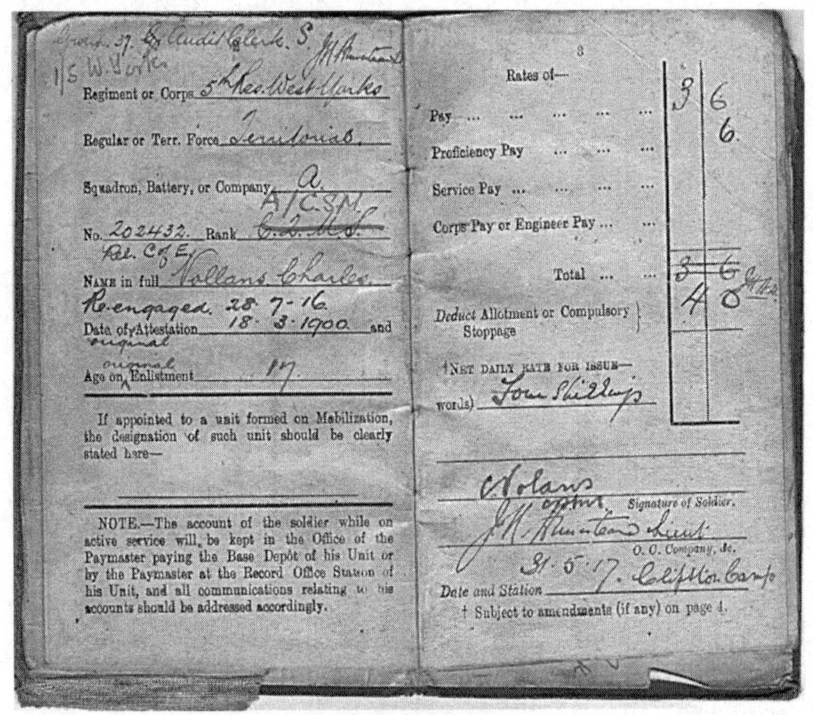

Regiment or Corps 5th Res. West Yorks

Regular or Terr. Force Territorial

Squadron, Battery, or Company a

No. 202432. Rank A/C.S.M.

Name in full Nollans Charles

Re-engaged 28-7-16.

Date of Attestation 18-3-1900 and

Age on Enlistment 17.

If appointed to a unit formed on Mobilization, the designation of such unit should be clearly stated here—

NOTE.—The account of the soldier while on active service will be kept in the Office of the Paymaster paying the Base Depôt of his Unit or by the Paymaster at the Record Office Station of his Unit, and all communications relating to his accounts should be addressed accordingly.

3

Rates of—	
Pay ...	3 6
Proficiency Pay ...	6
Service Pay ...	
Corps Pay or Engineer Pay ...	
Total ...	~~3 6~~ 4 0
Deduct Allotment or Compulsory Stoppage	

†Net daily rate for issue—(in words) Four Shillings

C Nolans Signature of Soldier.

O. C. Company, &c.

Date and Station 31-5-17. Clipston Camp

† Subject to amendments (if any) on page 4.

Charles' pay book

According to Charles' pay book, he was back with the Division, on the Western Front from 17th June 1917 with the Army Service Corps. At this time the Division was at Ypres and preparing for the Third Battle of Ypres

(Passchendale), which started in torrential rain on the 31st July.

The West Yorkshires were used as support until October 9th when the whole Division was involved in the final push that reached the top of Passchendale ridge on the 10th.

After losing half the manpower in the division it was pulled back to reform at Poperinghe.

During this time, as a senior NCO in the ASC, his role would have been to ensure all the equipment, food, ammunition, horses and fodder that was needed to keep the Division fighting was delivered to the troops at the front line. This was often under heavy shell fire.

They also had to arrange the rest camps for the troops when they came out of the line in the area near Poperinghe.

For the rest of the winter the Division was used to hold various sectors in the Ypres Salient whilst the Germans shelled the newly taken ridges.

***

CHAPTER 9

THE BATTLE OF PASSCHENDALE (3RD BATTLE OF YPRES)

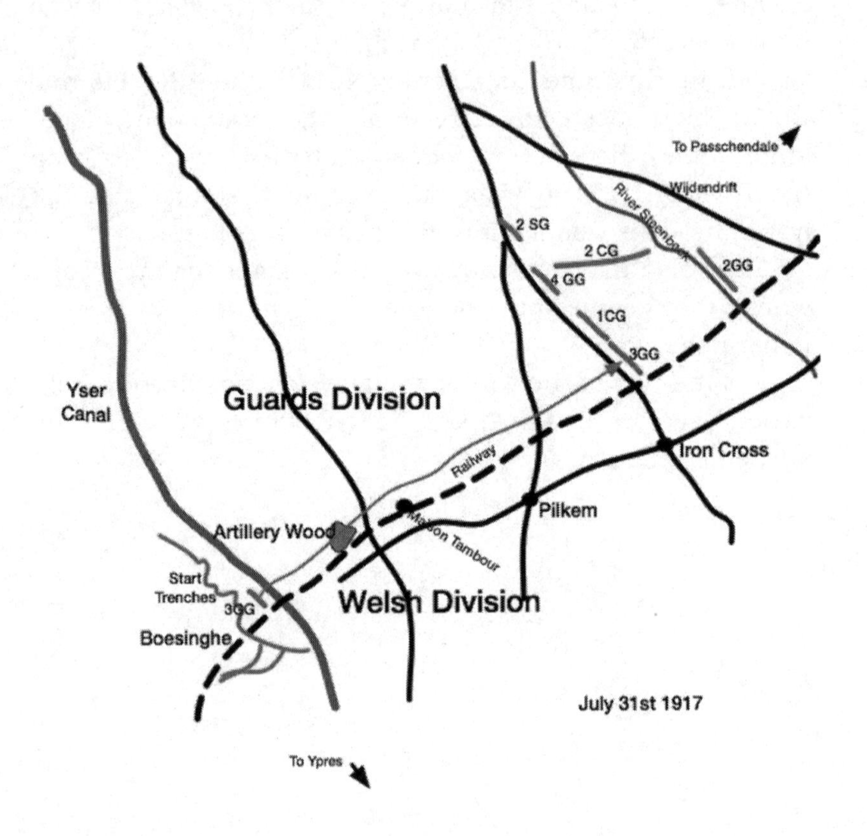

The Guards Division Assault

On the 2nd July, the Guards Division marched north to Herzeele between Ypres and Dunkerque. They were expecting to take part in a major attack in the Ypres salient. This attack was to be directed towards the high ground at the town of Passchendale, to the North of Ypres and was due on the 31st July. The intention was to drive the Germans from the high ground and relieve the pressure on the Ypres salient. They spent the next 2 weeks rehearsing the attack.

The Guards Division took over the northern sector of the salient with the French 1st Division on the left and the 38th Welsh Division on the right.

On the 13th the Battalion moved up to the rear trenches in the north of Ypres sector and spent a lot of time carrying ammunition into the front line under fire.

During this time a Guardsman in 4th Company was awarded the military medal for carrying a burning crate of Very lights out of a dugout saving the men taking shelter there.

On the 21st the Battalion took over the front line on the right of the Brigade sector near Boesinghe looking over the Yser canal towards the German lines. Their task was to explore the ground they were due to fight across.

1st and 2nd Companies held the front trenches with 3rd and 4th Companies in support.

For the next 5 days they were subject to heavy shell-fire. 27 men were killed outright and a further 11 men died of their wounds, with another 45 wounded and another 10 gassed. 7 men were sent to hospital with 'concussion', otherwise known as 'shell shock'.

On the 26th they were relieved by the 3rd Battalion Coldstream Guards and withdrew to a forest area to rest before the attack on the 31st.

The front line for the Allies lay on the west side of a canal. This was expected to be a difficult obstacle to cross under fire and the attacking Battalions had been practicing over a dummy canal and trenches. The plan was to cross and attack the German trenches on the 31st.

On the 24th British aircraft reported that there were few troops in the forward German lines. It was thought they had been pulled back to reduce casualties during the daily artillery bombardment.

A rescue mission from the 3rd Coldstream Guards was sent into the German lines on the left of the line, to bring back injured troops and they were able to complete their mission without being fired on. Consequently the Coldstream Guards sent out strong patrols deep into the German lines with a strong mopping up force and found them almost empty and were able to secure the frontline trenches without the Germans behind being aware of the invasion.

The Welsh division on the right, beyond 3rd Grenadiers Battalion, tried a similar raid and suffered from their patrols being captured or fired on from the rear because they had not put in a strong enough mopping up force to back up the assault troops.

The 3rd Coldstream held the German Front Line trenches without attack. German patrols were allowed into their old trenches and were then taken prisoner. This worked well until the 29th when a group of officers were taken but their NCO escaped and called in aircraft and shells on the invading Guardsmen.

The assault had the 3rd Guards Brigade on the left and the 2nd Brigade on the right.

Herbert's 3rd Grenadiers were again on the right of the 2nd Brigade supporting the 1st Scots Guards, alongside the neighbouring Welsh Division. These two divisions were separated by a railway line, running straight into the German lines and parallel to the line of the planned advance.

On the 30th July, the 3rd Battalion left their rest area in the forest and moved to the assembly area on the western side of the canal. They stopped in a field to the east of Elverdinghe about 400 yards from the canal, where they were given hot tea and rum.

As it became light at 5am and the Germans shelled the canal but not the assembly areas.

The Battalion approached the canal with 2 Company on the left, 1 Company on the right with Herbert's 3 Company as assault support to the forward Companies and 4th Company as carrying team to support the assaulting Companies.

Because the canal bridges had been blown the Battalions had to make their own by strapping petrol tins together to give the troops a footing in the mire of the bottom of the canal.

The barrage was intermittent so the troops crossed during the quiet periods in single file and did so without any casualties. They reached their first objectives at Artillery Wood without much difficulty, with 3 Company clearing German strongholds as they went.

Yser canal from the rail bridge

The second phase was more difficult. There were many concrete pill boxes armed with machine guns hidden within the lines. When the 3rd Battalion reached the second objective which was about 600 yards ahead of the first and parallel to the Plikem road, there were very few Scots guards there because so many had fallen forcing their way forward. Also they had to form a flank guard against pill-boxes set in the side of the railway on the right of the advance that ran from the canal towards the town of Passchendale, separating the Guards Division and the Welsh Division. The strongholds were particularly dense at a place called Maison Tambour. As the 3rd Grenadiers were coming up, 1st Company received 20 casualties from the machine guns in the Maison.

The railway track looking North, now a cycle track

3rd Company under Captain Neville was tasked with clearing this area to free 1st and 2nd Company and the remaining Scots Guards to allow them to advance and consolidate the second objective.

3rd Company was well practiced in this task and brought Lewis guns and grenades with them to take on the Germans and quickly suppressed this pillbox cluster.

The German defences along the railway were holding up the advance of both the Guards and the Welsh divisions. The Adjutant of the Guards Battalion went across the railway to the right planning to organise a combined assault with the Royal Welsh Fusiliers, on the railway bank defences. Unfortunately he was shot and was carried back to safety.

At this point a number of British spotter planes flew over and the troops identified themselves by waving large flappers above sheets laid on the ground.

The troops now started to advance on the 3rd objective; a line from a place called Iron Cross.

Progress continued to be very difficult because of the blockhouses on the railway.

3rd Company continued to hold the right flank, having now moved forward to Wood House, bringing their 2 machine guns to attack the pillboxes.

9 platoon, with Herbert, under Lt. Dunlop advanced but Lt. Dunlop was shot and killed. Capt. Neville then brought up 12 platoon to reinforce the advance and Lt. Braithwaite brought 11 platoon to hold the flank whilst the rest of the platoons advanced on the 3rd objective.

Capt. Neville, again noticed that the Welsh Division was still being held up by three pillboxes in the railway. Sgt. Browning and Private Baker from 3 Company led an attack on the pillboxes using hand grenades and despite being wounded they completed the mission killing 20 Germans and capturing 42.

3 Company managed to free themselves from the flank attacks and joined the line. Whilst they were preparing to advance, the 2nd Grenadiers arrived and passed through so Capt. Neville waited and collected his men but was then hit by a bullet.

At this time 4 Company arrived bringing up supplies. They were working as 5 parties of 20 men and a sergeant. Each man carried 4 stakes and 4 shells in a jacket, with a roll of wire in the early stages. Later they carried 2-3 water canisters in their shell jackets. One party did 5 trips of 1000 yards on that day, each taking 3 hours.

This phase of the attack stopped and 4 Company, who had not been directly involved as assault troops, were sent forward to hold the front lines for the 1st Scots Guards. The rest of the Companies took control of shell holes and residual trenches in the quagmire.

The cost to the 3rd Battalion was 2 officers killed, 4 officers wounded, 26 men killed, 113 wounded and 12 missing.

During the afternoon of the 1st August, in driving rain, the Irish Guards crossed the wilderness of shell holes filled with water and thick mud to relieve the Battalion. This allowed them to withdraw to the Forest area again for 3 days' rest. The rain continued to fall torrentially for the next month.

On the 4th August, they returned to hold the front line. As they entered the line there was heavy shelling killing the new 2nd Lieutenant of 3 Company.

A few days later they were relieved out of the line back to Herzeele for a week's rest before moving into the Corps Reserve whilst the 20th and 29th divisions took part in the next mass attack on the German positions.

In September the Battalion moved into one of the large camps (Eden camp) in the Corps' rear areas, but being close to the railway, they were subject to attack from German aircraft resulting in 40 casualties from bombing. They then moved to another camp (Rugby camp) but here, they were in range of the German guns so received regular shelling at night.

They re-entered the trenches in the Broembeek sector and were heavily shelled for the 4 days they held the line.

On the 20th September they were asked to extend and hold the line to the left whilst the 10th King's Royal Rifle Corps attacked into the German lines.

The next phase of the Third battle of Ypres was to be an attack across the Broembeek stream, parallel, yet again, to a railway line crossing the battlefield into the German lines.

Patrols had been out the week before the attack, to assess the stream and found it to be 20 feet across and 5 feet deep. However, on the day of the attack, the area had dried sufficiently for the troops to cross using the fallen trees, planks and duckboards without needing floats.

This time the 3rd Battalion was in the middle of the line with 1st Coldstream Guards on their left and 1st Irish Guards on the right.

On the 9th of October the attack started at 05.20. The 1st Scots and 2nd Irish took the lead, crossed the stream and reached the first objectives.

At 7.00am the Grenadiers and Coldstream advanced on their objectives, which they reached without much difficulty. Herbert's Company, now under Lt. Tetley, was deployed on the right as they approached their objective, Suez farm, near the small village Veldhoek.

On the way to this point, they took 2 field guns and 15 German prisoners.

The route ahead to the third objective, a line from the village to a cross roads, was defended by several blockhouses.

One of these was holding 3 Company back, so Lance Sergeant Rhodes advanced on his own and took the blockhouse, including 8 men who thought he was leading a platoon. For this attack he was awarded the Victoria Cross.

As the troops advanced, Germans hiding in dug-outs would come up and fire on them from behind. To counter this, 4 Company came up behind acting as 'moppers up' cleaning out the dugouts. Often the Germans coming out of the dugout would be confronted by only a 3 man team and would believe they could fight their way out, but the

British troops had become skilled at placing themselves in safe places to cover the dug-out entrance and then shoot the first German troops down as they left their strongholds. The rest of the dug-out would then surrender.

The third objective was secured and then reinforced by wiring parties from 1 and 2 Companies and two machine guns were brought up from the rear.

In the afternoon, German troops were seen approaching from the left at Panama house but were dispersed by the machine guns.

At dusk on the 9th August, the dead had to be buried.

The Battalion Chaplain, Capt. Phillimore was well liked by the ranks. He had been with the Battalion since it had let for France. He was always to be found up with the advancing troops.

Burying the dead in No man's land (Courtesy Imperial War Museum)

As Capt. Phillimore stood reading the service, shells were falling close around the burial ground, which was in the open. He was bare headed and when one of the men handed him a helmet he refused it with a shake of his head until the service was over.

During the 10th, the Battalion remained holding the newly captured line.

In the early hours, before dawn, there was a heavy barrage from the Germans and an attack was expected but failed to materialise. During the day, the Battalion pushed their line forward on the left and built up two strong-posts along the road towards Panama Farm.

The ground was a mess of water filled shell holes with slippery and crumbling edges.

During that night, the Battalion was relieved by the 4th Battalion Grenadiers and withdrew to rest.

This engagement had cost the Battalion 4 officers and 13 men killed, with 2 officers and 61 men wounded. 3 men were missing. They had captured 93 prisoners.

On the 17th October the whole Guards division was relieved and sent back to the rest areas. The division had lost 67 officers and 1899 men, about 20% of the force.

The Battalion moved into billets in Moule to rest and on the 21st October they were visited by the Duke of Connaught, and on the 25th by General Douglas Haigh.

***

CHAPTER 10

THE BATTLE OF CAMBRAI

After a few weeks rest and the arrival of fresh troops to replace those lost, the Guards division started moving south on the 10th November, marching at night in the hope of keeping the next planned attack secret from the Germans. The division moved slowly towards the town of Cambrai. To reduce the chances of gossip getting to spies in the country as they passed, the troops were not told where they were going or what the plans were. A story was circulated that they were going to relieve the French in the line. However, the troops suspected this to be false. Whenever they were sent forward as an attack, they would leave most of their spare kit behind the line so as to leave them free to move more quickly. For this 'Line Duty' they had been told to leave their spare kit in storage because 'there was little storage space in the French lines'.

On the 23rd November the Division reached Flesquires to the southwest of Cambrai and were sent forward to relieve two brigades of the 51st Division.

This march of 15 miles was in the dark and made worse because the position of the Brigade and Divisional HQ's had been given out incorrectly and the roads were blocked by large numbers of cavalry waiting for the expected breakout.

They reached the trenches at the southeast edge of Bourlon wood ready to attack the village of Fontaine Notre Dame.

The mood of the troops was low; the attack was across a front of 3800 yards but with only 6 Battalions. All the experience of the last year of campaigning had shown the survivors that success in attack needed a higher concentration of troops.

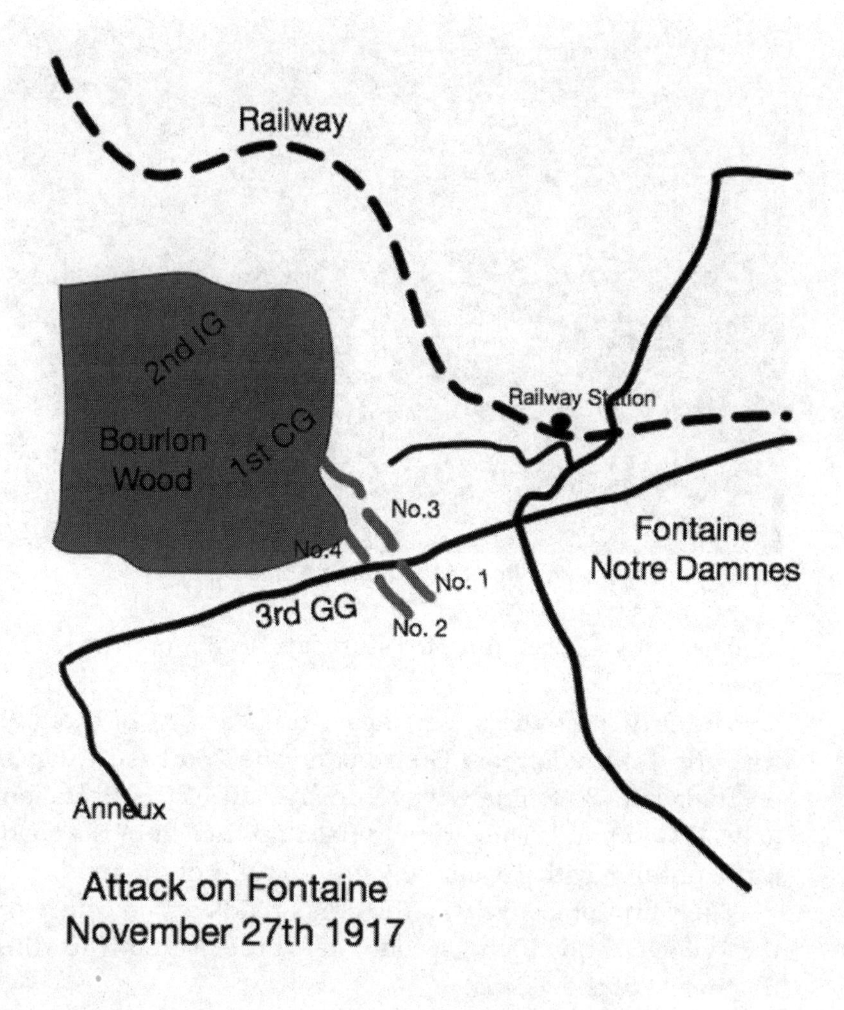

Attack on Fontaine
November 27th 1917

Another lesson of the last few years was that the use of heavy artillery made the ground difficult to cross during an attack and was thought to make the break out more difficult. For this attack, artillery was only to be used as a rolling barrage during the actual assault and tanks should act as a substitute to help the troops in close support.

Today: Road to Fontaine Notre Dame

The attack was due to start at 06.20 on the 27th November.

The 3rd Grenadiers were again on the right of the line with the 1st Coldstream Guards and the 2nd Irish Guards on their left. 3 Company were on the left of the Battalion as lead Company. They were to pass up the left of the road into Fontaine with 1 Company on the right of the road.

Their first objective was the cross roads at the centre of the village and their second was the station to the northwest of the village.

At 5.30 the Colonel and Intelligence Officer did a final round visiting the men.

At 6.20 there was a short artillery barrage, but, as had become usual, the expected tanks were late crossing the line so the troops advanced without them.

It was a cold night with a steady drizzle and poor visibility.

The 100 yards to the first objective in the village was over open ground under direct view, on the right, from the undamaged houses on the edge of the village, which, of course, made superb cover for the German machine gunners; and on the left from the trenches outside the village.

The wire in front of the trenches was uncut and without the tanks the two lead Companies suffered heavy casualties before they could break in and take the trenches.

3 Company Commander, 2nd Lt. Noare was wounded in the face at the wire and the Company was taken over by 2nd Lt. Knollys.

The tanks joined the Companies as they entered the town and with them they were able to reach their objectives by 8.30.

The houses on the sides of the road were held by machine gunners and were fought on both sides of the road, one by one. 3 and 4 Companies took the left side of the road and 1 and 2 Companies took the right, during which all the officers and most of the NCO's were killed or wounded.

Within the town, the men fought in small groups getting cut off as they moved forward. 12 men from 1 and 2 Companies fought through to the church where they met up with what was left of 3 Company.

3 Company now found themselves without any support on their right. They didn't know what had happened to the rest of 1 and 2 Company and so set up a defensive flank of 12 men and a sergeant with a Lewis gun.

They found a deep dugout under the Churchyard wall. There was a German hiding in the entrance who shot at anyone who tried to bomb the entrance, killing one man and wounding another. Since 3 Company was out of phosphorus bombs, they left a guard to prevent anyone getting out of the dugout and left it for later.

By now, the Grenadiers were surrounded and were receiving fire from all sides.

The tanks arrived in the centre of the town and assisted in clearing the streets and trenches but left the houses unsuppressed.

4th Battalion was sent up to support, with 1 Company joining the 3rd Bttn. and 2 Company joining the 1st Coldstream.

1000 German prisoners were taken but only 600 reached the divisional cage in the rear because there were not enough troops to supply full escorts, so many absconded on their way back.

The Battalion was holding a line through the centre of the village and Colonel Thorne set off back towards HQ to argue for more reinforcements.

On his way back he saw that the Germans had pushed an attack into a gap between the Grenadiers and the Coldstream Guards. He also saw that the German flank did not realise that the Grenadiers were there, so he organised his men to fire on them, driving them out until they returned with machine guns.

The Battalion was now very exposed, and a decision was made to fight back towards the start line.

By this time 50% of the Battalion were casualties and 9 of the 12 officers were killed or wounded.

Once the enemy were seen to be bringing in large numbers of troops, all the Battalions withdrew to the start line.

During the night the remains of the 2nd Brigade of Guards was relieved by Seymour's 1st Brigade and was withdrawn to La Justice.

This was seen as the first serious failure of the Guards Division in an assault and was blamed on the lack of assault troops and reinforcements. Because of their casualties, the whole Guards Division was then replaced in the line by the 59th Division.

Two days later, on the 29th they were called into reserve at Gouzecourt wood as support for the next assault but were not needed.

On December 1st they moved into reserve at Gauche Wood and moved forward into the chalk trenches in the wood during the evening. It was a very cold and frosty night and the troops complained of the cold as they had no blankets and no coats (having left them in storage for the assault). During the night they saw a group of Germans trying to rescue 2 field guns in front of their trenches and drove them off with rifle fire.

They stayed in the line under heavy bombardment but with no ground attack until they were relieved by the South African Regiment on the 4th December and moved back into a rest area.

Herbert is spared the frontline and the cold of Gauche Wood. Because there had been so many casualties the Battalion needed to be rebuilt. In these situations, experienced troops called 'Choice Men' were sent back to help form the new platoons and assist in training the men for life in the front line. On the 2nd December Herbert gets his papers to return to 'Tin City in England.

1918

In the spring the Germans made a massive attack out through the Somme splitting the line between the French and the British. The intention was to roll around the British and head for the channel ports cutting off access to supplies and reinforcements.

The 49th Division, holding the line in the Ypres sector, was mobilised urgently and the Army Supply Corps with Charles, was tasked to transfer the Artillery and an Ambulance Unit overnight from Ypres to Armentieres to help in stabilising the line. A few days later the whole

Brigade was returned to Poperinghe and re-entered the line to the west of Ypres across the Menin road.

Again the Germans tried to break through on the 25th April pushing up from the south of Ypres causing 18 officer and 557 troop casualties over two days amongst the 1/5th West Yorks. The attack was suppressed by 29th April and the last major German assault was over.

Charles' pay book suggests that he returned to England on the 21st May, after the end of the German assault and stayed there until the end of the war.

A combination of fierce fighting by the allies and a failure of the Germans to maintain supplies for their attacking troops once they had broken through, resulted in the attack slowing to a halt as the 4th Division of Guards joined the rush to plug the gap.

Herbert returned to France on 1st April 1918 with the replacement draft, sending a post card photo of himself to his mother.

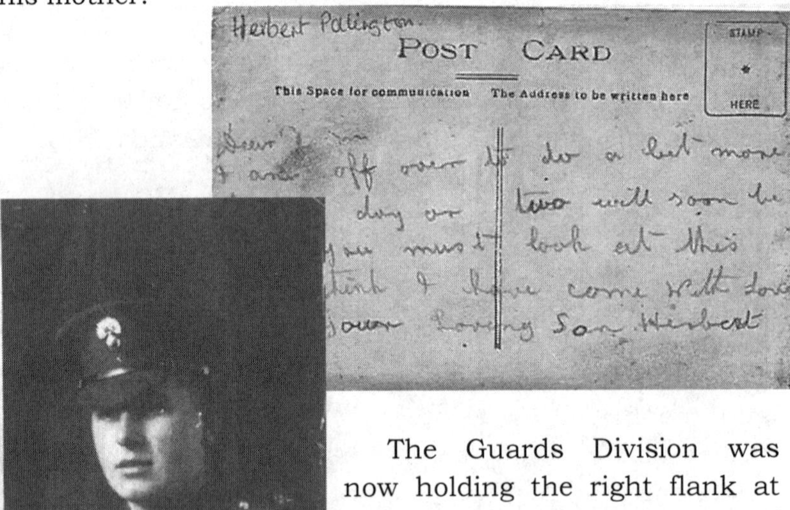

POST CARD

This Space for communication The Address to be written here

STAMP HERE

do a bit more
two will soon be
look at this
come with love
Son Herbert

The Guards Division was now holding the right flank at Ayette, at the northern edge of the Somme battlefield, just south of Arras.

The platoons of 3 Company were now under the command

of Lt. Geijer, Lt. Godman and 2nd Lt. Ball.

The Battalion spent the month of April in the trenches with a rotation of 3 Companies in the line and one in reserve swapping with periods in the support area. The days in the trenches were quiet but because they were under direct view of the Germans they were only able to make any repairs or improvements at night.

Herbert's draft arrived at the Battalion on 17th with 2nd Lt. Gibbon who joined 3 Company.

On the 25th they moved into the front line where there had been a change of design. The troops set up isolated front posts with a deep support line complex.

The frontline received heavy bombardment on the 27th before being withdrawn to reserve on the 28th.

During the first week of May, the Battalion was back in the line. The officers were out on patrol every night, lying out in No-man's land listening for activity in the German trenches. The rotation continued through May, during which the British artillery bombarded the rear areas of the German lines, concentrating on the assault areas, tracks and roads which resulted in retaliating fire on the Guards who spent their time deepening dug outs and building up the communications trenches.

On the 2nd June Lt. Cornish MC, the officer Herbert carried out from the Somme battle, and in so doing winning the Military Medal, returned to the unit, joining 1st Company.

On the 8th June the Battalion retired to La Baseque to billets and tents in the woods where they remained through June, training and practicing various new attack methods before moving to Ransart in early July and taking the right sector of the Divisional front.

Two Companies were holding the front line, one in support and one in reserve. The officers spent most of the nights in No-man's land watching the German line.

At the end of the month they were joined in the line by a number of officers and NCO's from the American Army who are learning the intricacies of trench warfare.

The Battalion retired into divisional support on the 30th July.

On the 4th August the Battalion moved into trenches at Adinfer with an American Company from 320th Regiment. During the nights they aggressively patrolled in No-man's land.

On the 6th 4 Company met an enemy patrol and managed to get identification information on the unit in front of them. HQ wanted more information so a large patrol from 4 Company was sent out on the 10th with a Captain Churchill from Brigade HQ. They slipped through the German wire and found a number of German sentries walking about on the tracks behind the wire.

Shortly afterwards they saw a German patrol coming forward. They appeared to be suspicious because they only communicated by whispers. 3 crawled forward then retired, apparently reporting that all was clear because they were followed by 30 to 40 Germans who stood up close together making a large target. When they were about 30 yards away the Guards opened fire causing several to fall. Although the Germans fired back there was no attempt to capture the Guards patrol and Churchill and his patrol returned with only one man wounded.

On the same morning, the Battalion Intelligence Officer and 20 men raided a German post under an artillery barrage. As the raid went over, the Germans escaped from their post but left documents about their unit. Again there was only a minor wound and the Battalion withdrew the next day, the 11th August to take billets in Saulty in the divisional rear area.

***

CHAPTER 11

THE BREAK OUT

The Allies planned to break through the new lines formed at the end of the German spring and July offensives. The intelligence gathered by the patrols along the lines had assessed the strengths and disposition of the German lines.

The continuous assaults against the German lines had ground down their reserves of troops and weapons.

The continued naval blockade of Germany, preventing food and materials reaching them had also reduced their fighting ability.

The American Troops were now starting to arrive in France although they were not yet active as an independent fighting force.

The 4th Army started in August by driving across the old Somme battlefield and pushing the Germans back.

With a very short planning time, the 3rd Army was tasked to continue to harass the Germans whilst they were occupied at the Somme in the hope that they could keep the Germans rolling back.

The Guards Division was tasked to join an attack to recover the Arras – Albert railway that had been lost to the Germans during their spring offensive.

On the 20th August, the 3rd Battalion and the rest of the 2nd Division of Guards loaded onto London busses and moved to assembly positions near Boiry St. Martin.

The plan called for an attack with three divisions. The 3rd Battalion was to support the 1st Bttn Coldstream on the left and 1st Bttn Scots on the right. They were to pass through when the 1st and 2nd objectives had been taken, and to move on to take the 3rd Objective. They were to have 8 tanks for each Battalion.

3 Company was commanded by Capt. Tufnell for this assault.

21st August 1918

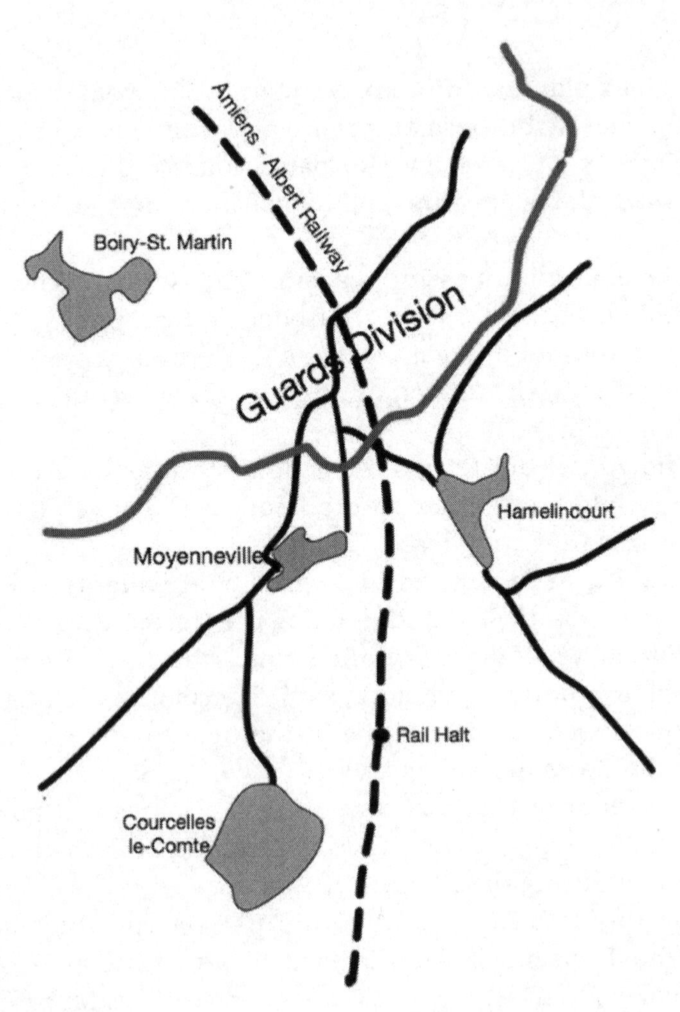

On the morning of the 21st there was a thick mist. Whereas this hid the attackers from the Germans, it also made it potentially difficult for the Battalions to find their way to the German lines.

The 3rd Battalion had had their breakfasts and had refilled their water bottles ready for advance when the thick fog came down.

At 4.53 am the artillery opened up their barrage. The commander of the tanks reported that his 8 tanks had been held up by a gas attack in Coseul Valley and hoped to be able to catch up by the second objective.

Number 3 Company under Capt. Tufnell advanced on the right with Number 4 Company on the left. Number 2 Company followed up in support and Number 1 as the reserve.

The fog was as thick as ever and made worse by the smoke shells fired with the barrage. Keeping the direction was difficult especially because the officers had to take their steel helmets and respirators off to use their compasses and again, the metal in the ground made compasses difficult to trust.

As they advanced, they found pockets of German machine gunners who had been missed in the first wave of the attack. 12 platoon from 3 Company captured 2 machine gun posts in the first objective. When they reached the second objective ready to assault the third, they found a cluster of German machine guns holding out. Although the Scots guards had taken both ends of the second objective trench, the centre was still held by the Germans.

The Scots, with the help of Number 1 Company, Grenadiers, cleared the rest of the trench, following which, the Battalion HQ was brought up.

All was confused. Tanks were moving around in the fog. Machine guns were firing in all directions. The HQ was attacked from the front by two platoons of the Scots Guards who mistook them for a German machine gun post.

At 7.30 the Battalion started to advance on the third objective. Number 2 Company advanced on the valley between the railway and the village of Moyenneville.

Two platoons of 3 Company and all of 4 Company were lost near Moyblain Trench. 11 platoon was also lost in the fog and found themselves moving back towards their own lines. 10 platoon (of 3 Company) found itself far to the south on the outskirts of Courcelles where they met another lost platoon from the 7th Bttn. Kings Light Infantry.

Working together they set off towards the final objective, the small halt on the railway line. As they progressed, clearing the dug outs on the road, they met and joined a tank that helped them along the way until they took and held the railway halt which they found contained a German aid post.

The War diaries record that these two platoons were the only units who reached their planned objectives for several hours on the whole of the front of the two Divisions.

When the Battalion Commander got word from 10 platoon, he sent Number 1 Company to support them with 2 machine guns.

There was no way of organising artillery support due to the poor visibility and all the Tanks were returning to base due to engine problems.

Whilst waiting for reinforcement, 10 platoon sent out patrols to explore their surroundings along the railway to the north. By 10am they had been reinforced and consequently the platoons attacked taking the German posts they had identified earlier.

Number 2 Company pushed onto the railway but was exposed to fire from the strongholds north of the Halt.

As 10 platoon and the supporting troops advanced along the rail, the fire from this area was suppressed allowing 2 Company to advance and take their objectives around the railway capturing 10 German machine guns and 60 prisoners.

As the fog lifted the attack continued across open ground under heavy fire but was successful despite the absence of artillery and tanks.

After dark, the fighting died down and the troops were re-supplied whilst the scattered platoons rejoined their Companies.

Patrols were sent out and found the German line about half a mile further on, reporting them to be very alert and in strength.

The independent nature of the battle, with platoons working co-operatively without strict instructions from the divisional HQ, was a new development within the British Army. As a result, the Battalion received complements from Divisional HQ, on the resourcefulness and skill shown by the troops.

The next morning there was a heavy barrage from the Germans over the whole Battalion area and a three-wave attack developed. The Battalion called down S.O.S. fire whilst the Companies on the front line open up with Lewis guns. The attack collapsed although they did succeed in getting into a trench on the right. Once the attack collapsed, this group of Germans had to retreat suffering heavy casualties.

Amongst the intelligence captured were the German orders for this attack, which showed that two Companies of Grenadiers had driven off an attack of over 4 Battalions of German troops.

On the 24th August the Battalion was pulled back to Ransart behind the lines. There the Companies were reorganised to reinforce those that had been hit hardest.

On the 1st of September the whole Brigade was put on notice for an attack and the Battalion moved forward to Hamelincourt, the village they had been approaching during the attack in August.

Here they set up bivouacs and collected wood to make fires to cook their dinners. Just as dinner was ready the Battalion was ordered to move 3 miles to the east to Saint Leger so they had to have a hurried meal before moving. The commanders were worried that the assembly areas for their assault would still contain pockets of German forces within the newly captured area so they decided to form up in the areas that had been taken a few days before and were known to be safe.

At 1 am on the 2nd September, the Battalion formed up and moved forward but with the HQ getting lost twice, the lead Company only arrived at 3 am. When the commander went round his troops at 4 am, there was no sign of three of the Companies, who did not arrive until the start time, due to them also getting lost on the way forward.

This was one of the new problems brought about by an open war. For 3 years the Battalion had known where they were going since they were taking trenches that had been held for months and even years. Now they were out in open country for which they had few maps.

This assault was led by 1 and 2 Companies and on reaching the objective; they found the Germans had moved on leaving behind a number of deserters but no fighting force. 3 Company, under Lt. Cornish moved up to hold the new line with 4 Company whilst the leading Companies moved forward across open country to the next ridge. This unopposed advance was very confusing to troops who had been trained in trench warfare.

By 2pm the troops had advanced 8 miles to the village of Boursies and the troops were exhausted but had suffered no casualties having only had a few shells sent towards them. The Battalion consolidated the position and then tried to rest.

At 5 in the morning the 3rd Guards Brigade passed through the Battalion to continue the advance leaving them to guard the right flank. Since they were on a hill and the visibility was good, only a few sentries were needed so the majority of the troops were able to rest.

On the 5th the Battalion moved up to the front line with 3 and 4 Companies in front with 1 and 2 in support. On the right there was a large gap full of wire that made up the old Hindenburg line and the British lines opposite it. This ran parallel to the direction that the Battalion was now trying to advance. The Germans were holding the canal about 2 miles ahead in the old deep defence trenches of the Hindenburg line.

Before advancing, the Battalion dug a complex of support trenches for defence. As they were finishing these, the Germans fired gas shells into the area of the support Companies 1 and 2. This gas was sneezing gas but then these stopped so the troops removed their respirators just as the Germans sent in Mustard gas mixed with explosive shells. 91 men of 1 and 2 Companies had to be led away blinded, along with 6 officers.

3 Company explored to the right about 500 yards and managed to link up with the King's Royal Rifles. What looked easy enough in daylight was made more difficult at night because the wire ran diagonally across the line to the Rifles making it impossible to move in a straight line. Also a compass was again useless because of the wire and there were no visible landmarks. By sending up Very lights from a stronghold, the troops managed to establish a thin line until they were relieved back to a support trench line on the 8th and then back to Lagincourt 4 miles behind, where 1 and 2 Companies received the bulk of a draft from England to make up their lost numbers. Because these new drafts were so new, 1 and 2 Companies were kept in reserve leaving 3 and 4 as the lead units for the next planned attack.

The Battalion was tasked with attacking the Canal du Nord. 3 Company with a platoon of 4 Company are to attack an area called Slag Heap near Havrincourt with the rest of 4 Company as support.

As the Battalion went into the line there was a raid from the Germans but with both the Welsh and Grenadier Guards being in the trenches the raid was beaten off easily. The Germans had been using the complex of old trenches that filled the area to sneak into the British lines so the Companies were on the alert for these attacks.

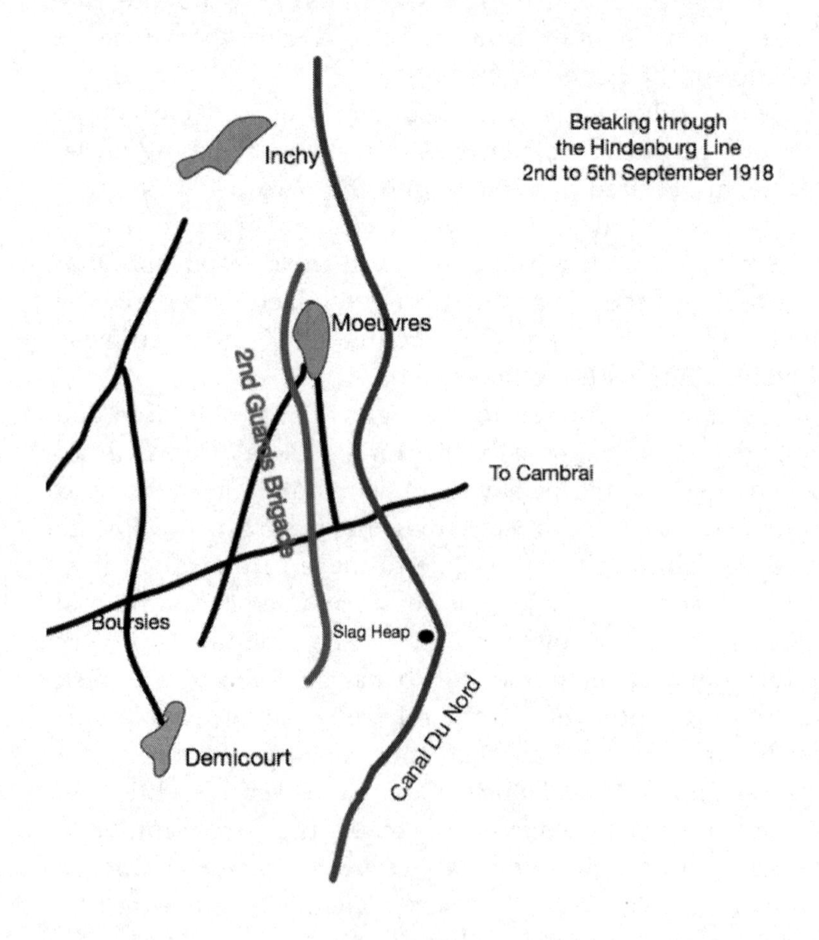

On the 27th the Battalion attacked northwards through the complex of wire and trenches, parallel to the line of trenches so that they could get through the wire by dropping into the trenches when the wire obstructed them.

Lt. de Geijer and 3 Company reached the slag heap at the corner of the canal as it turned west away from Havrincourt, and contacted the 1st Coldstream Guards. They established an aid post then started moving along two trenches when the Coldstreams reported that they were under heavy machine gun fire from their left flank. An NCO and a private slipped across the canal and captured it as well as an officer and 7 men.

According to a later letter to his parents, Herbert, with 2nd Lt. Gibbon and two other men entered a stronghold within the slag heap and captured 6 German troops sending them back towards the British lines. As the last surrendered German left, he took a bomb from his pocket and threw it at the Lieutenant; however they all had time to dodge behind a traverse and were saved from injury.

In the evening they pulled back to rest in Diognies a mile or so behind the line.

October 1918

In October the Germans were pulling back rapidly in both the French and British sectors. An attack under the King of Belgium threatened to cut off a large number of German troops and resulted in a very rapid withdrawal leaving enormous piles of stores behind them.

In this new open warfare, the Guards Division as a whole was moved steadily forward to areas where resistance was met when the retreating Germans stood their ground in prepared defences.

On the 8th, the Battalion moved to Premy Chapel to support an attack being made by the 62nd Division however they were not needed so moved on to Masnieres from where they could see the flames over Cambrai.

On the 9th they prepared for the next Guards assault on the railway line between Caudry and Cambrai which was expected to be very heavily defended with dugouts and fortifications set into the banks of the railway.

As the Battalion advanced. the leading Companies (1 and 2) with 3 Company in support, were fired on by one of their own aeroplanes and then the British artillery dropped shells onto them due to poor fire planning.

The first objective, a trench line from Niergnies to Seranvillers, was taken by 06.30 and found to contain only the casualties left from the bombardment.

There followed a rapid advance across the next planned objectives before moving on to landmarks chosen by the field commanders ending at the Cambrais –Beavois road with no sign of the enemy until this point where 2 Company came under fire from machine guns on the right of the line from the village of Igniel on the crest of the hill above the road.

Number 2 Company advanced up the sunken road to the village but came under harassing fire so they spread out into the fields. The German artillery dropped shells onto them, but the quality of the shells had noticeably deteriorated in that they didn't fragment and spread shrapnel on explosion and because of this there were very few casualties.

As night fell, the Battalion held a line on the edge of the village and across the adjacent fields with two Companies in support near Estourmel.

The next morning the 1st Battalion Scots Guards passed through to lead the next phase of the advance with the 3rd Battalion in support. As the situation was so dynamic, individual Companies were frequently transferred into different Battalions as and when they were needed, to replace casualties until the Battalions could be withdrawn to support areas to meet up with their reinforcements.

Number 3 Company with Herbert, was now on the right under Lt. Anson supported by 4 Company and had been taken under command of the 1st Scots Guards. 3rd Battalion's Companies 1 and 2 made up the reserve supported by 2 Companies of 1st Coldstream Guards sent up to replace the two Companies taken by the Scots.

On the 11th the 1st Guards Brigade passed through the line of the 2nd Brigade to drive forwards and the Battalion was reformed and sent into billets in St. Hilaire where they took advantage of the luxury of the German baths.

On the 13th, the 2nd Brigade passed through to continue the advance with the 3rd Grenadiers on the right and the 1st Coldstream on the left to support the 3rd Guards Brigade as it crossed the Selle River.

The Battalion moved up to the line and relieved the 2nd Scots Guards on the river.

1 Company sent a patrol across the river and capturing a German who confirmed the impression gained by the patrol that the Germans were disorganised.

A bridgehead was set up in the village of St. Python by 2 platoons of 4 Company with the rest of the Battalion forming a line on the river. The rest of the village was still under the control of the Germans who fired constantly on the Battalion.

Unlike the villages of the last few years, this village was still occupied. In St. Python there were 500 locals hiding in the cellars unable to escape. The Battalion found this a new and unusual problem that was highlighted when an 11 year old girl went on to the streets and was hit by German fire. A Guardsman went out and brought her back to shelter, but despite their attempts to treat her, she died of her wounds causing great distress to the troops involved.

On the 20th the 1st and 3rd Guards Brigades passed through to take the high ground to the east of St. Python and relieved the pressure on 3rd Battalion holding the line.

On the 22nd the whole Guards Division was taken out of the line for a week's rest.

***

CHAPTER 12

NOVEMBER 1918

The advance during November continued to be rapid. Because of the expected Armistice, and to save face, the German Army wished to prevent a major defeat in a standing battle so continued to pull away from the Allies.

Recognising the long term risk to peace that this might cause, the Allied High Command wanted to inflict a decisive defeat on the Germans in the field, to ensure complete victory for the Allies.

On the 2nd the Guards moved towards the town of Villers Pol as it was known the Germans would have to stand and fight to allow the rest of the army an ordered withdrawal.

On the 2nd, the Battalion left their billets in St. Python and moved, with difficulty, along the wet and greasy chalk track to Capelle where it bivouacked in the rain. They were told to dig in but found their tools too light to dig in the hard flinty soil of this area. There was some inbound fire from the German artillery but otherwise the day was fairly quiet.

On the 3rd they were issued with orders for an attack and drew their battle stores.

On the night of the 3rd November, the 2nd and 3rd Brigades moved into Villers Pol.

On the 4th, 3rd Battalion took up the assembly points at the rear of La Flaque Wood. They found the approach difficult due to the dense traffic. When they reached the village of Villers Pol, they were forced to stop because the bridge across the stream there was destroyed and had been replaced by a single plank which was made even more difficult by a combination of the Germans dropping gas and explosive shells into the area forcing the troops to wear their gas masks, and the area being under a dense fog.

Despite these problems the Companies reached their start points because of new detailed maps based on aerial photography.

For this attack, 3 Company were held in support with orders to follow on as 1(on the right) and 2 (on the left) Companies advanced through the Flaque Wood.

As the Germans pulled back to the North East, the chasing troops followed.

The Battalion HQ advanced and suffered a direct hit from a shell, but the ground there was so soft that when the shell exploded there were no injuries.

The right of their advance went well, supported by the 62nd Division.

However on the left there was strong resistance. Number 1 Company attacked under the cover of some wildly thrown smoke grenades, which burst in mid-air startling the Germans who withdrew down their trenches.

As they advanced they had to cross thick hedges that the Germans made good use of as defensive points. Again 1 Company suffered at the hands of the Germans but they managed to suppress the defenders.

On the left, a gap had appeared between 1 Company and 2nd Grenadiers into which the Germans were trying to push. The Machine Gun regiment held them back until 3 Company moved in to reinforce the gap.

The German troops opposite 2 Company found their southern flank unprotected as 1 Company pushed forward and withdrew leaving the 1 Company able to take most of the village of Preux. The only part still in German hands was a trench on the southern edge of the village from which the Germans poured enfilade fire on the Company as they crossed an open slope resulting in the last Company Officer being wounded; however the attack was completed by the Company Sergeant-Major who took the trench, driving the Germans out of the trenches but not out of the houses that lay behind them until 10pm when, in the dark, the houses were taken and the next jump off line was consolidated.

The stretcher bearers had suffered heavily during this attack and Capt. Phillimore, the Padre, helped the Medical Officer, attending the patients who were scattered around the battlefield because of the lack of bearers to bring them into the aid station.

On the 5th the 3rd Guards Brigade passed through while the Battalion remained at Preux collecting salvage.

On the 7th the Battalion was placed on the left of the attack but because of the state of the roads, could not get to the start line until 20 minutes after the assault had started. However again, the Germans had pulled back and the objectives were taken without resistance.

In the afternoon of the 7th a German messenger was captured carrying orders for the German rear guard, to be held at all costs whilst the main body of troops withdrew through Maubeuge to set up a defensive line.

On the 8th, the CO of 3 Battalion was asked if his troops were fresh enough to advance that night, towards Maubeuge along the road. He declared that they were and so in a very dark night they moved along the road, exposed above the surrounding fields with Companies in the ditches on either side of the road.

Setting off at 10 pm they crossed mine craters and reach the Maubeuge citadel at 4 am on the 10th taking the whole town and Citadel.

According to Capt. Phillimore's letter to Herbert's mother, he was point man of the lead platoon entering Maubeuge and indeed was the first British soldier into the town.

There was no opposition during the approach and three officers and 35 men were taken as prisoners.

Above: The Guards at the southern 'Porte du France' destroyed by the Germans during WW2.
Below: The northern 'Porte de Mons' at Maubeuge today

On the way 4 Company got within 150 yards of a German gun before its team took it away at the gallop.

In the town, the only civilian the CO could find was a priest who told him that the Germans had evacuated just a few hours before the Grenadiers arrived.

During the following day the inhabitants of the town reappeared greeting the Battalion as liberators.

On the 11th the Armistice was announced and the Battalion held a thanksgiving service.

***

CHAPTER 13

TO GERMANY

On the 18th November the march to Cologne started. The weather broke and there were several days of rain so the men were often soaked before they reach their billets.

Initially the troops were greeted as heroes by the civilians, being met with flowers and speeches.

As they entered Flemish Belgium, they came to areas that had never had troops before and here the population was distrustful of the troops.

When they reached German soil, the British Troops were expecting a hostile reception.

The civilians were very wary of soldiers and seemed surprised on being treated courteously, which resulted in a positive response from the civilians.

It was a surprise to the British troops that the civilians were not aware that their own army had been defeated.

The 3rd Battalion reached Cologne on the 15th December taking the last section by rail.

The troops found that the population was concerned about the anarchy that was developing in the country and looked on the British troops as a stabilising force.

Through December and January the troops settled into a more ceremonial role. They supported the civil authorities in controlling the returning German troops who felt that their country had betrayed them. Quite quickly, the novelty of acting as conqueror palled and the troops were keen to return home. In the meantime they had comfortable barracks, were warm and well fed and spent their free time enjoying winter sports such as skating.

The Battalion was notified that they were due to return to England in February.

The accident happened on the 31st January. It is described in a letter written by the padre, Capt. Phillimore, to Herbert's mother on February 4th 1919.

The troops had been skating on a pond near the barracks. The Padre and the Doctor had been on the ice and noticed that it was a bit thin.

An hour after they had left, Herbert was skating when some German children fell through the ice. Herbert went over to the hole and succeeded in bringing between 2 and 4 children out. The letter said that it was difficult to know how many for sure due to the Padre not knowing the language.

Whilst getting the last child out Herbert fell through the ice into the water.

Some German civilians came to the Barracks to get help but by the time the rescue party got to him he had died, possibly of cold or perhaps drowning.

He was buried with full military honours on the 4th February with the service lead by the Padre. There were wreaths from the Mayor of Cologne as well as other town folk.

2 days later, the Battalion entrained to return to England.

Herbert's mother received a letter from Buckingham Palace expressing the King's regret at her loss in such circumstances after surviving the war. These letters are stored in Herbert's 1914 Christmas Box along with his last picture postcard of himself taken just before he returned to France for the last time.

Charles Volans was demobbed in York in 1919, keeping his Military Coat since he preserved the receipt that would get him £1 refund were he to return it. He obtained a job as a senior clerk for a piano Company although his preserved letters suggest that he continued to be restless and frequently argued with his employers.

BUCKINGHAM PALACE

22nd. February, 1919.

Dear Sir,

The King has heard with much regret of the death of your son, Guardsman Pollington, who, after coming through four years of the War with honour and credit, has now with a true British spirit of nobility given his life in an attempt to save some Germans from drowning.

I am commanded to convey to you His Majesty's sincere sympathy in the cruel fate which has deprived you of a gallant son, whom you were hoping shortly to welcome home.

Yours very truly,

Clive Wigram

W.T. Pollington Esq.,
Victoria Avenue,
Thirsk,
Yorkshire.

20454 GUARDSMAN
H. POLLINGTON M.M.
GRENADIER GUARDS
31ST JANUARY 1919 AGE 22